FOREWORD

Long before I became a television chef I was foremost a teacher—first at my own cooking school and then at the California Culinary Academy, a school for professional chefs. What was important for me then was to teach Chinese cooking techniques so that my students could gain a fundamental understanding and appreciation of one of the most ancient cuisines in the world.

Today, with Jeremy Pang's masterpiece *Essential Chinese Cooking*, the author has successfully distilled the essence of how to make delicious authentic Chinese dishes through simply explained techniques. In this book every essential aspect is covered, every recipe is written with clear directions on how to prepare and cook each dish, while Jeremy's distinct voice (and sense of humor) fills it with his personal experiences and observations. I love how helpful substitution suggestions for harder to find ingredients are provided, while practical tips on technique give you the know-how you need to cook with confidence, as if Jeremy was right beside you. I also love the way in which traditional Chinese recipes have been given new life with unusual ingredients or sauces, while Martin Poole's mouthwatering photos make me want to run into the kitchen to try them out.

I am certain you will find *Essential Chinese Cooking* as enlightening as I do and will agree that it belongs in the kitchen of anyone with an interest in cooking.

KEN HOM

PHOTOGRAPHY BY MARTIN POOLE

ESSENTIAL CHINESE COOKING

**AUTHENTIC
CHINESE RECIPES,
BROKEN DOWN
INTO EASY
TECHNIQUES**

JEREMY PANG
OF SCHOOL OF WOK

quadrille

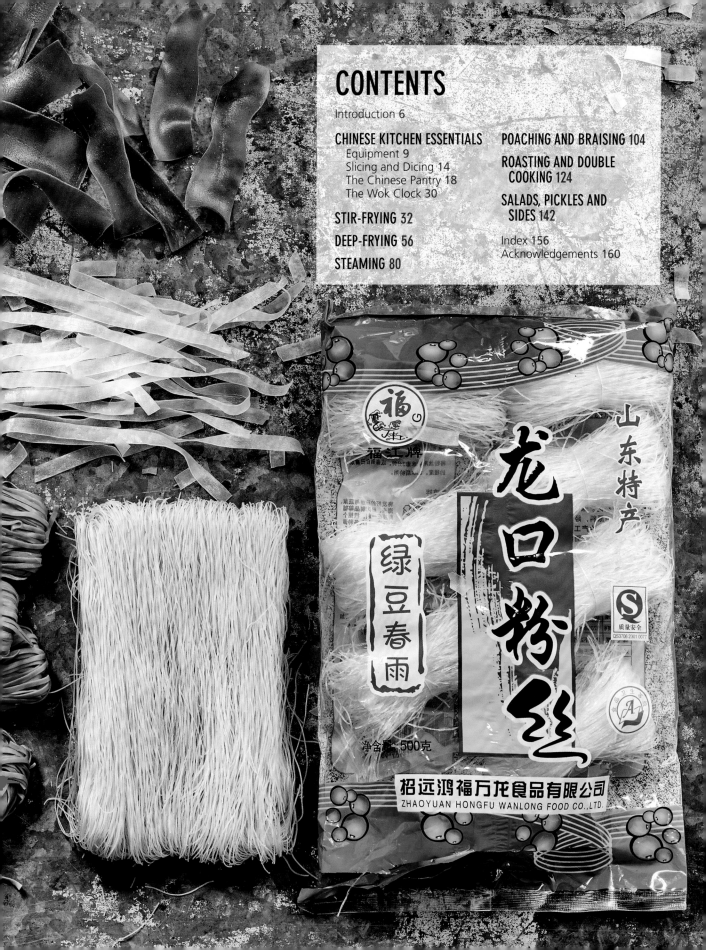

CONTENTS

Introduction 6

WE CHINESE HAVE A KNACK OF KEEPING OUR COOKING A SECRET. IT'S ALMOST AS IF, WHEN THE CHINESE FIRST STARTED MIGRATING ACROSS THE WORLD, WE HELD A CULTURAL PACT—A UNANIMOUS UNDERSTANDING THAT WE SHOULD OPEN CHINESE RESTAURANTS, PERHAPS, BUT NEVER GIVE AWAY ANY OF THE SECRETS OF CHINESE COOKING. I SUPPOSE IT MAKES SENSE. AFTER ALL, WE WOULD ONLY BE GIVING OUR RESTAURANTS COMPETITION IF WE DID SO ...

Although my dad was a brilliant home cook and inspired my love for food, he flatly refused to teach me his "Chinese kitchen secrets." Rather, he would insist we children sat and watched while he skipped across the kitchen with cleaver, board, and wok and got to work. Twenty minutes later (and far too fast for us to work out what happened) dinner would be on the table. After a few minutes of silent scoffing, he would make us guess exactly what he had put into each dish. Although we'd be none the wiser as to how dinner was made, this daily palate training kept our taste buds constantly excited, and has definitely led me to where I am today.

Being British-born Chinese, I've been lucky enough to experience and enjoy the wonders of both cultures and—while my Chinese language skills are terrible, to say the least—I am proud to say I've retained this crucial part of my Chinese cultural identity, our love of eating and cooking. In 2009 I decided to share this love by starting the School of Wok and teaching people how to cook Chinese food in their own homes. Truth be told, I was a little fearful that that my ambition would be frowned upon by almost all the Chinese restaurateurs in the country. A Chinese cooking school certainly wasn't part of the unspoken arrangement our families and ancestors all seemed to have made! However, it's now clear to me that the two aren't mutually exclusive—there are times when you want to eat at home and others when you just don't.

And besides, Chinese food really isn't as daunting to cook as it may at first seem. Like any cuisine, when examined closely and from a basic level, the patterns and techniques it follows quickly become obvious. In the last five years—teaching in completely different environments and with all different types of stove, heat, woks, and knives—I have learned more about Chinese cooking than ever before, and it is through these experiences that I have come to understand what I believe to be its core cooking techniques. These may take a little patience and practice to get the hang of at first (but doesn't anything in life worth learning?); however, once mastered, they will give you the confidence to create authentic Chinese dishes in any home kitchen environment.

The aim of *Essential Chinese Cooking* is to help unravel and demystify the true techniques of Chinese cooking to get you cooking and eating authentic Chinese food at home. Whether you want a simple one-wok-wonder with a bowl of rice on the side or are feeling brave enough to cook three or four dishes to create a feast to impress your friends and family, through my recipes, descriptions, and directions, I hope to be able to help you achieve a wonderful Chinese homecooking experience.

CHINESE KITCHEN ESSENTIALS

EQUIPMENT: THE CLEAVER

WHAT IS THE DIFFERENCE
BETWEEN A CHINESE CLEAVER
AND A CHINESE CHOPPER?

ARE THEY THE SAME THING?

ARE THEY JUST BIG WESTERN
BUTCHERS' KNIVES WITH
CHINESE WRITING ON THEM?

DO I REALLY NEED ONE TO
COOK CHINESE FOOD?

Well, none of these statements are necessarily correct. Much like Western and Japanese chefs' knives, there are hundreds of different types of cleavers (a composite term for all of the above) that all have different uses within the Chinese cooking world. And while, no, you don't necessarily need one to make Chinese food, they are an interesting and efficient piece of equipment to have and enjoy should you decide to make the purchase. They come with their own history and their own specific technique, different from the Western knife, making them a unique and useful addition to your kitchen equipment.

Cleavers come in many different shapes, sizes, thickness, and weights—from general slicers to duck slicers, and general choppers to *kau gong* (heavyweight choppers). There are even cleavers made specially to create perfectly round dim sum pastries. The difference between a cleaver and a chopper is the weight of the knife itself and the materials it's designed to cut through.

For those looking to make their first cleaver purchase I would recommend starting with a "general slicer." General slicers tend to have a nice thin blade, with a well-balanced weight and a fairly sized grip or handle. These types of cleavers are designed for slicing and simple vegetable chopping, not for chopping through bones. If you want to chop through bones, it's best to leave that to the butcher, or invest in a chopper: a cleaver specifically made with enough weight on the top of the blade to withstand the extra force required to cut through tougher materials.

When it comes to using your cleaver, efficiency is key. Slicing is by far the most efficient way of prepping your food. A good slicer has an incredibly sharp, thin blade with a slightly thicker top edge to allow you to use your nonknife hand to push down on it. When we slice a vegetable or a piece of meat, we tend to use a good 70% of the blade; therefore, the whole blade has been sharpened in order for it to be used efficiently. This differs from chopping, where one point of the blade is used. See pages 14 to 17 for a detailed guide on how to slice vegetables and meats.

EQUIPMENT: THE WOK

Back in the old days woks used to be made of cast iron, and even the thinner woks would be extremely heavy to handle. These days, the best stir-frying woks are made of thin carbon steel. They conduct heat incredibly well, but more importantly, due to the thin metal, they also lose heat very quickly, which suits stir-frying perfectly (see pages 32 to 33 for more details and advice on how to supercharge your wok cooking skills).

Traditional woks are round-bottomed, and for good reason—the circular bowl assists with circulation of heat through the pan, which is essential for stir-frying or tossing ingredients through the wok. Unfortunately it is difficult to use traditional round-bottom woks on a modern stove, which is where I would definitely recommend opting for a flat-bottom wok instead. While there are plenty of flat-bottom woks on the market, my best tip is to look for a flat-bottom wok that still has "curvature" and maintains a smooth bowl shape even though it has a flat bottom. If your flat-bottom wok has a shape much like an upside-down roof, then I'd recommend investing in a new one.

Nonstick woks were invented for ease of cleaning and have the benefit of simple maintenance. Although they may not be as hardwearing as traditional carbon-steel woks, with new technology they are becoming more resistant to damage from everyday use and utensils. Personally, I still much prefer to use the traditional carbon-steel woks as they give off that extra smoky, caramelized stir-fry flavor when cooking. If it's easy maintenance you're after a nonstick wok will serve you well, however if you really want to get your stir-fries closer to your favorite Chinese restaurants and takeouts (if not better), then get yourself a carbon-steel wok and take the time when you've first bought your wok to season your new toy as explained below.

SEASONING THE WOK

Most carbon-steel woks will come with an antirust layer on the wok to prevent it from corroding when sitting on a shop shelf, but seasoning the wok is essential to creating a natural "nonstick layer" on the wok. Follow the steps overleaf and look after your wok and it should last a lifetime.

CREATING A NATURAL NONSTICK LAYER:

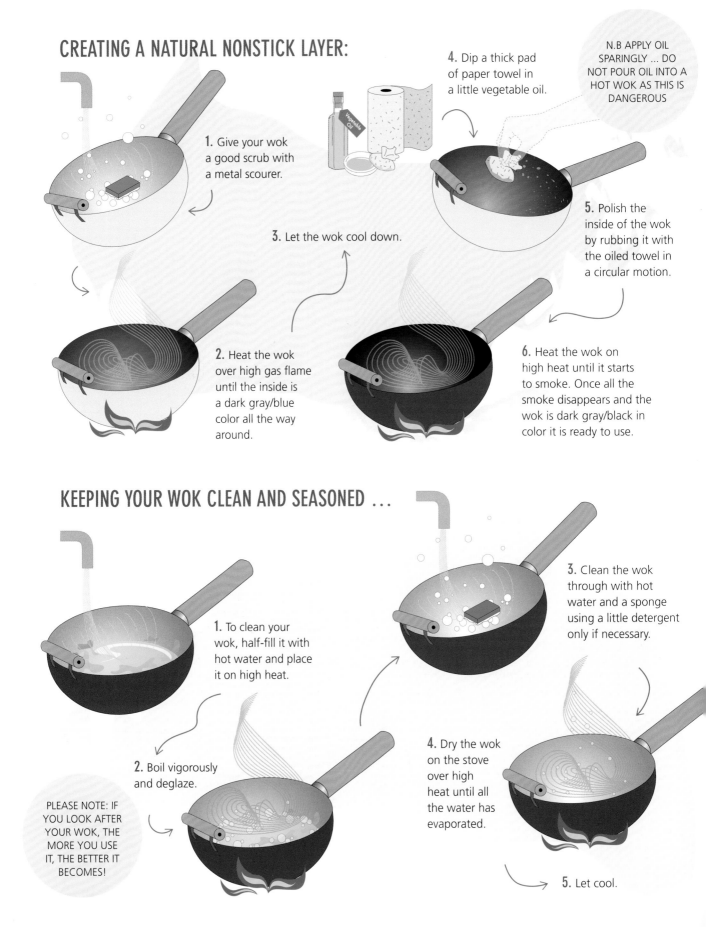

1. Give your wok a good scrub with a metal scourer.

2. Heat the wok over high gas flame until the inside is a dark gray/blue color all the way around.

3. Let the wok cool down.

4. Dip a thick pad of paper towel in a little vegetable oil.

N.B APPLY OIL SPARINGLY ... DO NOT POUR OIL INTO A HOT WOK AS THIS IS DANGEROUS

5. Polish the inside of the wok by rubbing it with the oiled towel in a circular motion.

6. Heat the wok on high heat until it starts to smoke. Once all the smoke disappears and the wok is dark gray/black in color it is ready to use.

KEEPING YOUR WOK CLEAN AND SEASONED ...

1. To clean your wok, half-fill it with hot water and place it on high heat.

2. Boil vigorously and deglaze.

PLEASE NOTE: IF YOU LOOK AFTER YOUR WOK, THE MORE YOU USE IT, THE BETTER IT BECOMES!

3. Clean the wok through with hot water and a sponge using a little detergent only if necessary.

4. Dry the wok on the stove over high heat until all the water has evaporated.

5. Let cool.

OTHER EQUIPMENT

The following equipment and accessories are also incredibly helpful when cooking in a Chinese kitchen and can be found in almost all Chinese grocery stores around the world. All of these accessories will come in different shapes and sizes, depending on what you require.

WOK LADLES

If you want to get serious with your wok cooking, certain accessories help. Wok ladles, much like Western ladles, are made to hold a certain amount of liquid in the bowl of the spoon. The end of the spoon, however, is positioned at a slightly more obtuse angle to allow for easy stirring and to maintain a good circular movement when it comes into contact with a wok full of ingredients.

WOK SPATULA

Full metal spatulas can also be found with a similar angle to the wok ladle. They are incredibly helpful if you want to get completely underneath your ingredients without breaking them apart. Some people find spatulas easier to use than ladles when folding through food, as they allow it to be more delicately handled.

WOK MESH STRAINERS

Wok mesh strainers, or "bamboo spiders," as I like to call them, are giant, flat strainers with large, weblike metal mesh surfaces and long bamboo handles. The weblike mesh helps to fish out food from a wok or pan when deep-frying or blanching ingredients.

COOKING CHOPSTICKS

Wooden cooking chopsticks are incredibly useful when cooking Chinese food. They essentially act as wooden tongs, but are a little more versatile as they can be used to test oil heat too. Large wooden chopsticks are also very useful for deep-frying, as the extra length keeps you farther away from the hot oil in case of spitting.

STEAMERS

Steamers come in several different forms, from stainless-steel bottoms with glass or metal lids to the more traditional bamboo steamers. You can also find stainless-steel steamer stands that sit inside your wok—these are great for steaming large items such as whole fish.

Bamboo Steamer: The biggest difference between a bamboo steamer and a stainless-steel steamer is that the bamboo lids of the steamer collect condensation between the layers of bamboo, acting as a "sponge" and preventing excess water from dripping back into the food after the steaming process has finished.

Stainless-steel Steamer: Stainless-steel steamers usually come with a large saucepan at the bottom to hold large amounts of water and therefore have the ability to steam for long periods of time. If you have a stainless-steel steamer and are worried about condensation and dripping from the lid, the trick is to wrap the lid with a clean dish towel to absorb the excess moisture.

Stainless-steel Steamer Stands: If you want to save space in your cupboards, a small steamer stand and wok lid are all you need to create a steamer using your wok. Simply fill your wok halfway up with hot water, place your steamer stand in the middle of the wok, then carefully place your plate of food on top. Finally, cover the wok with a suitable high-level lid, which can be found in most Chinese grocery stores.

SLICING AND DICING

Chinese cooking terms in general are much less technical than the brunoise, macedoines, and juliennes of what is considered classical Western cooking, but the principles of slicing, dicing, matchsticks, and general preparation are just as important—if not more so, given the importance of preparation in this type of cuisine.

Our terms of cooking are, in fact, very literal. When we want something finely sliced, we say it's finely sliced. When we need it in big chunks, we cut off a big chunk and show the shape and size to our peers. And when it comes to cooking processes, we call a stir-fry a stir-fry, because the food should be continuously moving (in the right way, of course … see pages 32 to 33 for tips and technique). With such quick cooking processes, Chinese cooking can almost be split into ninety percent preparation, ten percent cooking. And with such emphasis on preparation, it is crucial to understand how to use your cleavers properly to slice, dice, or chop in the most efficient way possible, as the success of your dish is reliant on this preparation of ingredients.

Preparation is the key to unlocking successful Chinese cooking. For example, when I am at home cooking a meal for my friends and family, the first step I tend to make is to prepare and slice all my key ingredients for the meal. I always start with the basic ingredients i.e. ginger, garlic, and scallions, or onions. Once everything has been sliced and diced, I then organize myself and get ready to cook, starting with the slowest cooking techniques (roasting, braising, and poaching), while leaving the quicker cooking methods (stir-frying, deep-frying, and steaming) to the last 15 to 20 minutes just before serving. Even when cooking just one dish, the same process can be used—see page 30 for more details.

Additionally, when considering the different cuts, shapes, or sizes, keep in mind that everything you prepare for one dish should be a similar size in order to cook quickly and maintain the texture of the ingredients. Here are some tips on how to improve your general knife skills and therefore become much quicker at cooking your home Chinese meals.

THE "CRAB"

Gaining confidence in holding a large cleaver or knife is all down to practice. We have two hands for good reason—the nondominant hand is what we call a "five-legged hermit crab"; where the three middle fingers become the front legs, and the little finger and thumb act as the back legs.

1. The golden rule is never to allow the back legs to stray ahead of the front legs!

2. The hand structure is "crablike" as the fingers are always bent, never straight. This creates a stable guide for the dominant hand to start slicing.

3. The slicing movement needs to follow long, stroking movements in a down and forward motion.

4. Once the blade is completely flush with the surface of the board, push forward and slice.

! TIP: Never leave a gap between the blade and the board when slicing— firstly, it will allow your fingers to get underneath, and secondly, it will not slice through your ingredients properly!

PREPARATION AND PRESENTATION

SLICES

Present the crab (with your nondominant hand) lightly on top and in the middle of the ingredients you wish to cut. Push down and forward with the cleaver to slice in half. Once halved, place each half securely on the board and slice through the ingredients to the desired thickness using a down and forward motion with your knife.

MATCHSTICKS

Take your prepared slices and lay them flat on the board lengthwise. Using a down and forward rocking motion, lift up your wrist while pulling back slightly to slice the ingredients into large sticks.

DICE

Take your prepared matchsticks and turn them ninety degrees. Using the same rocking motion, starting down and forward and picking up your wrist, cut the sticks into large dice.

FINE SLICES

When finely slicing, you must be confident enough to hold the flat part of the cleaver or knife much closer to your crab hand. With the side of the knife leaning against the front knuckle of your crab hand, follow the same down and forward motion described above to achieve fine slices.

FINE MATCHSTICKS

Take your fine slices, lay them in a neat line flat on the board lengthwise (without towering them up too high), and slowly push down and forward, lifting up your wrist when coming back up in a rocking motion to cut the slices into fine matchsticks.

FINE DICE

Take your fine matchsticks and turn them ninety degrees. Line them up neatly and, once aligned, use your crab hand to hold the matchsticks in place lightly. Use the rocking motion, starting downward and forward, to cut the fine matchsticks into fine dice.

MEAT-SLICING TECHNIQUES

CHUNKS
Hold on to the piece of meat with the back legs of your crab (thumb and small finger) on the side of the meat and the front legs of your crab in a straight line. Using long sawing motions with the knife hand, cut the meat into roughly ½-in (1-cm) chunks.

STRIPS
Fine strips are the quickest and simplest way to cut into your meat for simple stir-fries. Hold on to the piece of meat with your crab hand as when cutting into chunks and slice into strips no more than 1/16 in (2 mm) thick.

FLATTENED SLICES
Carefully lay your crab hand over the meat. Place the blade of your cleaver at a slight angle, roughly ⅛ in (3 to 4 mm) from the edge of the meat, then slice through the meat on the diagonal in long, sawing motions. Once you've sliced all the pieces, flatten them with the side of the cleaver to tenderize the meat and create the perfect pieces for a stir-fry.

HOW TO INFUSE FLAVOR INTO MEATS
There are plenty of ways to infuse more flavor into meats. This method creates extra surface area across a piece of meat without the need for accessories such as meat hammers.

1. Place the meat in the center of your board. Hold the tip of your cleaver with your crab hand.

2. Rock the cleaver up and down in a fast rocking motion and run the blade up and down the piece of meat lightly, taking care not to cut completely through it. This will make lots of little cuts across the meat, opening up the surface area to allow as much of the marinade to penetrate as possible.

3. Once you have made plenty of scores along the meat, slice into whatever shape you desire and then flatten with the side of the cleaver before marinating.

BUTTERFLYING

The large surface area of a slicing cleaver is great for butterflying as it is easy to lay the side of it horizontally on top of the piece of meat.

1. To butterfly the meat, lay the side of the cleaver on top of the center of your chosen cut of meat and push down slightly with the thumb on your knife hand. This will create a slight "groove" in the piece of meat.

2. Now lightly lay your crab hand on top of the other side of the meat. In one slow, long, slicing movement, slice the "groove" of the meat down toward you, keeping your knife in a horizontal position (so as to cut into the meat, but keeping it intact and in one piece).

3. Once you have made the first slice, move your crab hand and pick up the top part of the meat that has just been sliced into, and then place your knife back into the groove and repeat the above step. However, this time, pull the meat upward with your crab hand while you are slicing into the groove. You will see the meat starting to unravel or "butterfly."

4. Continue to slice through the groove, pulling upward, until you have reached the end of the piece of meat, but do not cut through it. You should finish with one piece of meat.

5. Now turn your piece of meat and repeat steps 2 to 4 on the other side of the meat to open it up fully and finish off the butterflying movement.

THE CHINESE PANTRY

Having a well-stocked pantry is paramount to learning about any new cuisine. Aside from all the wonderful implements and utensils such as woks or cleavers, I've always thought that the modern Chinese pantry shows just how versatile our cuisine can be. With its use of fermented soybean-based sauces, flavored oils, and China's long history of noodle making, rice agriculture, and food preservation, there is a world of pantry ingredients out there.

The problem with such a huge choice of ingredients is that it can become a little daunting. As I'm a big believer in starting small and building onward and upward, I would like to touch on just a few pantry ingredients at a time.

"LEVEL 1" INGREDIENTS form the basic level of a Chinese pantry that I believe are essential to our cuisine. Once you understand where these ingredients come from and the general principles of how they are used, you will notice that tens of different recipes follow the same simple rules. These pantry ingredients are more often than not found in most Western grocery stores.

Suggested recipes for Level 1 ingredient use: Garlic and Egg-Fried Rice; Steamed Trout with Chili Bean, Garlic, and Ginger Oil; Barbecued Hoisin and Cola Ribs (see pages 34, 94, and 141).

"LEVEL 2" INGREDIENTS delve further into the realms of Chinese cooking. These ingredients should start to give you an idea of new flavors and textures, while working to balance quantities of certain sauces or different suggested soaking times for thicker noodles. These ingredients may be easier to find in more specialist Asian grocery stores than in Western grocery stores.

Suggested recipes for Level 2 ingredient use: Flash-Fried Cabbage with Dried Chiles and Sweetened Soy; Braised Curried Squid; Pickled Lotus Root and Spinach (see pages 39, 110, and 150).

Throughout the book, there are also suggested "SWAPSIES" ↰ as there are often times that you cannot find certain more unusual ingredients. The true essence of Chinese food is this; with these core techniques set out in the book, and a stock of basic Chinese sauces in your pantry, you will always be able to cook delicious Chinese meals and will not always have to rely on the traditional ingredients. The point is not to be intimidated by ingredients. Feel free to try out the alternative "Swapsies" and see how close you can get to the essence of the real thing!

NOODLES

Noodles are considered to be symbols of good luck as they represent long life in Chinese tradition. It is important to make sure the noodles are cooked properly in order to maintain their structural integrity and add a textural component to your dish. Dried noodles are amazing pantry ingredients as you can essentially make a whole meal in a matter of 10 to 15 minutes without much more than a bit of technique and a sauce or two.

Noodles can be bought either dry or fresh in most grocery stores these days. There are certain differences between using freshly packaged noodles and dry packages of noodles. Personally, if I have the choice, I'd rather use dried noodles as there is no added oil or extra flour used to keep the noodles separated.

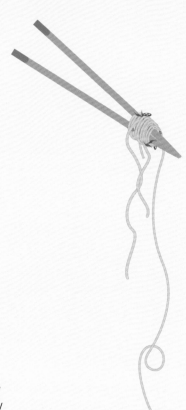

FRESH NOODLES

Fresh noodles bought from Chinese grocery stores are often coated in a bit of oil or excess flour to keep them moist and separated. Before using fresh noodles make sure to separate the noodle strands carefully using your fingertips. They are then ready to use however you wish to cook them

DRIED NOODLES

Dried noodles are an essential part of a Chinese pantry. They can be stored easily in a cool, dry place and will last for quite a few months. To make the most of any pack of dried noodles, follow the directions below:

1. Put your noodles in a large mixing bowl

2. Cover the noodles fully with boiling water and leave for 3 to 5 minutes (depending on the thickness of the noodles). Note: If you leave the noodles in the water too long, they will become too soft and will not have the "al dente" bite that they should once cooked.

3. Once the noodles have been soaked and separated nicely (essentially once they have lost their package shape), immediately drain them in a strainer and run them through cold water.

4. Cover a tray with a clean dish towel and place your noodles on top.

5. For best results, let the noodles dry for 20 minutes before use. Alternatively, to speed up the drying process, pop them in a fan-assisted oven with the fan function on the lowest possible heat, or no heat at all if possible. This will dry your noodles out within 5 to 10 minutes.

6. The noodles are now ready to cook in any way you like (whether boiling adding to a soup, stir-frying, or deep-frying)

! **TIP:** When looking for a good pack of dried noodles, if the noodles are packaged in "nests," ensure you can see that the strands of noodles are indeed separate even if tightly woven. The little pockets of air show that they will separate easily when soaked.

LEVEL 1

Egg noodles
Egg noodles are usually made from wheat flour, water, egg, and oil. As well as acting as an extra binding agent, the egg adds an extra depth of flavor and color.

Rice vermicelli / Singapore vermicelli
Rice vermicelli can be found in many grocery stores both fresh and dry. These noodles need very little soaking if bought dry and must be well dried and separated before stir-frying; otherwise they become very soggy and start to break up in the wok.

LEVEL 2

Chop suey/Chow mein noodles
For those who cannot eat egg, chop suey or chow mein noodles are a great alternative. These noodles are also made with wheat flour, water, and oil and get their distinct yellow color from traces of the alkaline lye water. Depending on thickness, these noodles should only require 3 to 4 minutes of soaking in hot water if bought dried.

Hor fun rice noodles
Hor fun noodles can come in all different shapes and sizes. They are essentially slightly thicker versions of rice vermicelli. The thickness provides a totally different texture and when soaked properly (usually around 5 to 8 minutes) or bought fresh, they can feel almost a little slippery in texture. Hor fun noodles work well with caramelized sauces such as black bean or pad Thai.

Mung bean vermicelli/Glass vermicelli
All types of bean vermicelli can be found inAsian grocery stores. They are good used in stir-fries and are also great for warm and cold salads as they have a slightly jellylike texture and feel fresh and delicate on the palate. They can also be used as light alternatives for soup noodle dishes.

Sweet potato noodles
Sweet potato noodles come in different forms, sometimes as vermicelli (thin) or flattened, more like hor fun noodles. They also have a glassy, jellylike texture and are light on the stomach. Sweet potato noodles are fantastic for bulking out both cold and warm salads and work well with the earthy texture and flavors of ingredients such as mushrooms or crispy tofu.

RICE

There are so many different grains of rice around the world. Below are some of the main grains used in Chinese cuisine. The use of each type of grain has also been adapted depending on availability (and therefore popularity) among the many Chinese cultures that exist throughout the world. Each type of grain may require more or less water due to the amount of starch they contain and how well they absorb water. Whatever rice is used, it must be washed well and soaked in some cases before being cooked, in order to remove any excess starch and keep the grains separate.

JASMINE RICE

Jasmine rice sits halfway between a long-grain and a medium-grain rice and tends to be used to make steamed "Thai-style sticky rice." This rice can be used for steaming and frying; however, when making fried rice using jasmine rice grains, I would suggest using roughly 10% less water than normal.

Suggested water-to-rice ratio:
- 1 : 1 water-to-rice in small quantities (i.e. for 1 or 2 cups of rice)
- 1.25 : 1 water-to-rice for more than 2 cups of rice

BASMATI RICE

A long-grain rice often used in Indian cooking. This rice is also ideal for steaming in advance to use for fried rice, as the grains tend to keep separated better than other types of rice such as Thai-style jasmine rice.

Suggested water-to-rice ratio:
- 1 : 1 water to rice in small quantities (i.e. for 1 or 2 cups of rice)
- 1.5 : 1 water to rice for more than 2 cups of rice

AMERICAN LONG-GRAIN RICE

This rice has a distinct texture and bite to it and is often used in restaurants and takeouts for fried rice, as it tends to be slightly cheaper than the alternative basmati or jasmine rice. However it can sometimes feel almost a little too dry and may not provide as "fluffy" a texture as jasmine or basmati when steamed.

Suggested water-to-rice ratio:
- 1 : 1 water to rice in small quantities (i.e. for 1 or 2 cups of rice)
- 1.5 : 1 water to rice for more than 2 cups of rice

GLUTINOUS RICE

Glutinous rice, as its name suggests, is much stickier than the average rice grain and has a definite "gluey" texture to it when cooked. This type of rice is used widely within Southern China and Southeast Asia for both savory and sweet dishes. It is also ground down into flours for types of dim sum pastries and desserts. When using the rice it is advisable to soak it for at least 2 hours before cooking so as to allow as much moisture to be absorbed by the grains as possible.

Suggested water-to-rice ratio:
- Roughly 0.7 : 1 water to rice

SIMPLE BOILED/STEAMED RICE

Ingredients
1 cup rice
1 cup cold water
¼ tsp salt
½ tsp granulated sugar

Preparation
- Place the rice in a saucepan with a tight-fitting lid.
- Put the saucepan under cold running water and wash the rice well to remove excess starch.
- Once washed, pour over the cup of cold water and place the pan on the stove.

Cooking
- Cover the saucepan with the lid and bring the rice to a boil over medium heat.
- Once vigorously boiling, lower the heat to a simmer, replace the lid to cover, and let simmer for 10 minutes, until the water level is the same as the top of the rice.
- At this point, turn off the heat and let the rice rest for another 10 to 15 minutes keeping the lid on at all times.

Serving
- Use a wooden spoon to fluff up the rice grains before serving.

SAUCES, DRY AND PRESERVED GOODS

The "sacred soybean" has an obvious significance in Chinese cuisine, with fermented soybeans used in many of the sauces that stock up our pantry. Alongside all the spices and sauces that we use to create these unique flavors are hundreds of preserved ingredients that you can find in Chinese grocery stores, and this is where I believe the true fun starts! Understanding some of these key ingredients is a great place to begin your Chinese cooking adventure.

SAUCES LEVEL 1

1 Light soy sauce
With less sugar present in light soy sauce than dark soy, this should be used to add saltiness to a dish and generally for seasoning and marinades.

2 Dark soy sauce
The added sugar content in Chinese dark soy sauce gives it a "caramelized" flavor that is great for adding color and depth to a dish.

3 Oyster sauce
Made from a high concentration of oyster extract, oyster sauce should be used sparingly (1 to 2 Tbsp at a time) to add savory flavor to stir-fries, marinades, and stews.

4 Chili bean sauce
Fermented fava bean, soybean and chile are the main components of chili bean sauce, which will lend a dish an umistakable depth of heat, saltiness, and savory flavor.

5 Hoisin sauce
Popularized by duck and pancakes, hoisin sauce has a great texture that comes mainly from toasted fermented soybeans as well as plenty of sugar, balanced with a bit of salt. The texture and sweetness of hoisin is great for balancing sour flavors in sauces.

6 White rice vinegar
Rice vinegar will lend a dish much-needed sourness with a subtle savory note, which works perfectly with stir-fry sauces and sweet-and-sour dishes.

7 Sesame oil
Sesame oil gives a dish that classic "Chinese food" smell and should be used at the start of your dish in a marinade or at the end of a dish to finish it off with a toasted, nutty flavor. Sesame oil is rarely used for frying as it has a very low smoking point.

DRIED AND PRESERVED FOODS LEVEL 1

8 Dried shiitake mushrooms
These meaty mushrooms add texture and bite to any dish. As they are dehydrated, they absorb a lot of moisture and flavor when soaked.

9 Bamboo shoots
In the West, bamboo shoots most often appear in canned form. To get rid of the slightly metallic taste, it's best to blanch the bamboo shoots in hot water for 5 to 10 minutes, or try to find fresh or vacuum-packed bamboo shoots instead.

10 Water chestnuts
These provide a great crunchy texture to dumplings, stir-fries, or stews.

11 Deep-fried shallots
Used as a garnish, or as a key ingredient in rubs or savory crumbs, fried shallots not only add crunch to a dish but also have a great sweet/savory flavor.

12 Sesame seeds
A unique ingredient used to add texture to a dish without overpowering other flavors.

13 Cornstarch
The main type of flour used in Chinese kitchens (easily replaced with potato starch) to thicken sauces, tenderize meats, or make crispy batters.

SAUCES LEVEL 2

1 Kecap manis
This highly caramelized Malaysian sweet soy sauce is great for creating sticky sauces to coat and cling to other foods. Its molasses-like flavor and texture work perfectly with natural sour flavors such as tamarind.

2 Chili garlic sauce
Essentially a chile and garlic puree, this is great for adding to dipping sauces or for using as the base of a stir-fry.

3 Chiu Chow chili oil
This oil is good for red-hot, oily stir-fries, but the best bit is actually the chili layer under the oil, which holds all the sweet caramelized flavor of the preserved chiles from the slow-frying process used to create it.

4 Sriracha chili sauce
A Thai-style hot chili paste made with garlic, vinegar, salt, and sugar. Its smooth texture makes it perfect for sauces that need a smooth finish.

5 XO sauce
A modern invention from Hong Kong and southern China that is made from a base of chile and garlic but includes a high percentage of dried shrimp and scallops, which provide a rich seafood flavor to any dish.

6 Sweet chili sauce
Sweet chili sauce is not just a dipping sauce for shrimp crackers! Its jamlike texture is perfect for thickening sauces without having to use cornstarch or starch and it has a great balance of sweet, spicy, and sour.

7 Sesame paste
Sesame paste is the epitome of savory. With a peanut butter-like texture it works very well in salad dressings as well as adding a lovely consistency to sauces.

8 Sambal sauce
A Malaysian-style chile, tamarind, and onion jam. Fantastic on its own on the side of fried rice or soup noodles, and works well in stir-fry recipes as well.

9 Yellow bean paste
A great substitute for hoisin sauce for those not keen on the sweetness of hoisin, but wanting a similar texture.

10 Plum sauce
Often confused with hoisin sauce, plum sauce is definitely more like a thick, sweetened version of sweet chili sauce and is actually made from fermented plums.

11 Shaoxing rice wine
The flavor of shaoxing rice wine resembles a savory dry sherry or brandy. It is often used in stir-fries to add a certain aromatic flavor and in marinades to help tenderize meats.

12 Chinkiang black rice vinegar
Vinegar made from fermented glutinous rice husks (which are black by nature). This vinegar has a unique depth of sweet, sour, savory flavor.

13 Red rice vinegar
Much like black vinegar, but with a more subtle, less caramelized flavor.

DRIED AND PRESERVED FOODS LEVEL 2

14 Preserved black beans
Providing a strong, assertive flavor to any dish, Chinese black beans are actually salted, dried soybeans, rather than beans. When soybeans are preserved and salted in this way, the salt is extremely prominent.

15 Shredded cloud ear fungus
With its jellylike feel once soaked but surprising crunchy texture, shredded cloud ear fungi are great for salads, rustic stews, or stir-fries.

16 Dried golden lily mushrooms
One of the many types of dried mushroom that add meaty textures to a dish without the use of meat itself. When soaked, they have a stringy feel to them that works well with noodles and steamed dishes.

17 Pickled Tianjin cabbage
A special type of cabbage fermented and pickled in salty garlic solution. Its strong taste is used to add flavor to soups and steamed meats or in simple dishes like fried rice.

18 Pickled bok choy
Brined in a similar way to pickled cabbage, the vinegary kick of pickled bok choy is good as a side to soupy noodles or added to fried rice or other stir-fries.

19 Silken tofu
Whether firm or soft, this tofu is very delicate with a great "melt-in-the-mouth" texture.

20 Salted eggs
The Chinese have eaten salted duck eggs for centuries. Once steamed, the chalky texture of the yolk can be used to create unique Chinese sauces.

21 Red fermented tofu
With a unique texture much like a creamy blue cheese, fermented tofu is often used to thicken and provide a silky-smooth finish to sauces.

22 Dried yellow soybeans
Soybeans in their dry form are great for adding to vegetable broths and provide complex depth of flavor.

23 Tamarind concentrate
A natural sour flavoring used in a lot of Southeast Asian cuisines and adopted by emigrant Chinese as an alternative to the vinegars used in mainland China.

24 Evaporated milk
An unusual addition to a Chinese pantry, evaporated milk is prized for its silky texture and is used to enrich sauces.

25 Panko bread crumbs
A Japanese ingredient in origin, panko bread crumbs add a delicately crunchy texture that works well with the myriad Chinese deep-fried foods.

26 Black sesame seeds
Simple seeds that lend a dish color, texture, and flavor.

27 Salted soybeans
When yellow soybeans are preserved in a salty brine solution, they become soft. Mash them to form pastes or add a unique salty thickness to a stir-fry sauce.

28 Dry unsweetened coconut
Dry unsweetened coconut is used in many cuisines throughout Asia. Its unique bite when dried is also very versatile. When toasted it turns a beautiful golden brown and is great for garnishing dishes.

SPICES AND COOKING OILS

Spices and cooking oils form an essential part of Chinese cooking. The former give many of China's most iconic dishes their trademark flavors while the signature Chinese cooking technique, stir-frying, would be impossible without the latter. Although five-spice may be the most commonly known spice in Chinese cuisine, there are many other noteworthy spice influences from other parts of the world that find their place in the Chinese kitchen.

SPICES LEVEL 1

Chinese five-spice

Chinese five-spice does indeed have five spices in it, or possibly even more at times, depending on who has made it! The main ingredients of five-spice are star anise, cinnamon, clove, and fennel seeds. The fifth ingredients can be anything from Sichuan pepper through to mandarin peel, ginger, garlic powder, or all of the above. Most importantly, these individual spices are all very strong in flavor, so use it sparingly!

Dried red chiles

Dried red chiles would have found their way over to China from Central and South America. They add a great punch to oils and act as a great base flavor to many stir-fries and stews.

Chili powder

While Western China may be most famous for its use of chiles, a wide variety of chili powders are used throughout China to strengthen sauces and give depth of heat to all types of dishes.

SPICES LEVEL 2

Sichuan peppercorns

This citrusy flavored husk of a berry, derived from the prickly ash bush in northwest China, leaves a numbing feeling on the tip of the tongue. It is one of the main forms of heat in Sichuan-style cooking and is a feature of many five-spice mixes.

Star anise

A dried star-shaped fruit from southwest China, star anise gives dishes a strong, sweet anise flavor. It is a main component of Chinese five-spice.

Cinnamon sticks

Although cinnamon is often used in Western desserts, if you bite directly into a piece of raw cinnamon, it will leave more of a "hot," "spicy" flavor in your mouth. This quality works perfectly in five-spice and can also help bring a sweet heat to a stew or broth.

Cloves

Also a key component of five-spice. The menthol or anise flavor of cloves can be quite strong and occasionally overpowering. Use sparingly!

Fennel seeds

Fennel seeds also have an anise flavor that works well with the rest of the above spices.

Mandarin peel

Adding dried mandarin peel to broths, sauces, or rubs will give them a unique, complex, bitter-sweet flavor.

Cumin seeds

Although not used in every region of China, the use of cumin seeds reflects the influences of India and can be found in certain parts of west and southern China.

OILS

Vegetable oil, Sunflower oil, and Corn oil

All these oils are commonly used in Chinese kitchens as they all have high enough smoking points to stir-fry and deep-fry at high temperatures. They also provide that immediate seal, which is most important for these quick cooking methods.

Peanut oil

Peanut oil also has very high smoking point and is therefore great for stir-frying or deep-frying. Bear in mind that it must be used with special care if cooking for people with peanut allergies.

Canola oil

Canola oil has a high smoking point and is ideal for stir-frying as well as for those who are highly health conscious, as it has the lowest saturated fat content of any of the cooking oils.

Rice bran oil

This oil is used a lot in Japanese cooking and in high-end Chinese cooking. Rice bran oil has an extremely high smoking point and therefore provides the perfect temperature for deep-frying. However it can prove quite expensive and is therefore used less often in households.

✳ THE WOK CLOCK

NOW THAT WE'VE
COVERED HOW TO USE
YOUR CLEAVERS, SLICING,
DICING, AND PREPPING YOUR
INGREDIENTS, THE NEXT
HURDLE IS UNDERSTANDING
HOW TO ORGANIZE YOURSELF
BEFORE YOU START TO COOK.

I often get asked how Chinese takeouts manage to serve up a number of dishes so quickly. Aside from the amazingly powerful equipment they have access to in their commercial kitchens, there are also some basic organizing techniques they use which are invaluable when it comes to keeping your cooking quick as well as your kitchen clean and tidy. One specific technique, which we call "The Wok Clock" and have developed and use daily at the School of Wok, will help you to take that leap forward by setting up your ingredients in order of use before you start to cook. By doing this, you won't even have to look back at the recipe while in the throes of cooking, saving yourself time and energy without ever having to sacrifice the cooking of your ingredients while you reread your recipe.

Once you have prepared all your ingredients, place them in their cooking order on a large round plate, beginning at 12 o'clock and working your way clockwise all around. It's that simple! This organization is not exclusive to wok cooking (the "wok clock" is just a simple phrase to remember); whether you are cooking a stir-fry or a slow-cooked curry, it works. The photo opposite, for example, demonstrates a wok clock set up for our School of Wok Stir-Fried Sichuan Chicken, see page 48. Once you get in the habit of organizing your ingredients in this way you'll find cooking as a whole to be a much neater and more straightforward process, freeing you up to experience the joys of preparing dishes and learning new techniques rather than constantly scampering to consult your recipe books.

BALANCE IN CHINESE FOOD

Chinese food is all about achieving a balance of flavor, texture, and color—whether you are serving one plate or several plates of food. While there are certain individual dishes that can touch almost all your flavor sensations at the same time, to master the true skill of Chinese cooking, the more challenging scenario is being able to select a number of dishes which touch all or most of the basic tastes (SWEET, SOUR, SALTY, SAVORY/UMAMI, SPICY, AND BITTER), a good combination of textures (CRISPY, SOFT, MELT-IN-THE-MOUTH, OR SUCCULENT) and are in turns meaty and rich, light, and fresh.

If your meal covers all of the above, you are almost there! The last part of the puzzle is making sure that there is a good balance of colors, bright, dark, neutral, which is what really plays a big part in the presentation of Chinese food. Remember, we also eat with our eyes! If you are able to understand this balance of flavor, texture, and color, you are definitely moving toward becoming a seasoned Chinese cook.

STIR-FRYING

Stir-frying, as its name suggests, is the motion of frying something while continuously stirring or circulating heat, and it's that heat that is all-important—stir-frying is all about **WOK HEI**, or "wok's air" in English. Think of it as the "height of fire," or the level of heat. It's said that Chinese cooks have good **WOK HEI** if they have a true understanding of the heat of their wok and how to handle it in all situations. Unfortunately I have discovered that very few recipe books actually mention the importance of the height of fire, which strikes me as leaving out a crucial part of the recipe. A stir-fry's success is based on the cook's **WOK HEI**!

A stir-fry is, in its nature, incredibly quick to make—your average chicken stir-fry should only take about five minutes. This is why you slice or dice your ingredients into small pieces: it speeds up the cooking process and allows the "height of fire" to do a quick, but precise job of cooking and sealing your food.

Many Chinese chefs insist that the golden rule of wok cooking is to have an extremely hot wok and a high source of heat, and I agree. Cooking on high heat seals the flavor in your ingredients and keeps in moisture. However, domestic kitchens don't have huge wok burners or even necessarily gas stoves, and it takes an extremely brave (or slightly crazy) home chef to be confident dealing with a smoking-hot pan straightaway.

So perhaps the key to mastering **WOK HEI** at home is not how to heat up your wok, but actually how to cool it down. The methods outlined here will help you cook quickly, but also safely, keeping the cooking heat high but giving you a bit more cooking time so your stir-fry will be crisp and delicious—and most of all, not burned!

STIR-FRY: THE GOLDEN RULES

1) BE ORGANIZED
Always make sure you have all your ingredients 100% prepared and organized before you start your cooking! Stir-frying is very quick and it will get very hectic if you are not organized before you start. The easiest way to organize yourself when stir-frying is to present all your ingredients—from harder vegetables, to meats, to softer vegetables—in a clockwise order around a plate so that you do not have to think or even look at the recipe once you start. This is what I refer to as a "wok clock" (see page 30 for more details).

2) USE OIL SPARINGLY
Add a maximum of 1 Tbsp of oil before cooking, and then add oil bit by bit (½ Tbsp at a time) as and when you need it. You need just enough oil to cover the bottom of the wok. If too much oil goes into the wok at the start, the first ingredient you add will absorb it all and your stir-fry will be greasy.

3) WAIT FOR THE SMOKE
Oil should be smoking hot before you add any ingredient to the wok. However, if your wok is still smoking once the ingredients are in the pan, it needs cooling down (see below).

4) LISTEN FOR THE SIZZLE
Your wok must always make a sizzling sound. At times you may need to cool your wok down; however, one thing is certain when stir-frying; NEVER LOSE YOUR SIZZLE! No sound? Turn up the heat.

5) HARDER VEGGIES GO IN FIRST

Some ingredients take longer to cook than others, like harder vegetables and chicken, for example. Put these in the wok first to ensure they cook through.

6) MEAT TIMINGS

When stir-frying, all meat should be finely sliced or thinly diced to cook quickly. If you are looking for a quick "one-wok-wonder" stir-fry, the meat generally will enter the stir-fry between the harder vegetables (e.g. carrots, broccoli) and the softer vegetables (e.g. choi sum, bean sprouts). If, however, you would like to try the more professional route, you may blanch the meat in hot oil thereby prefrying the meat in the wok for 1 to 2 minutes and removing it. This extra step will help to seal in the meat's moisture and flavor, and the meat can then go back in just at the end of the stir-fry, before adding the sauce.

7) ONLY USE HIGH-HEATING OILS

High-heating oils such as vegetable, sunflower, corn, peanut, and canola oil smoke at roughly 375°F (190°C), which is much higher than olive or sesame oils. Wok cooking requires an extremely high heat, so make sure you only use these high-heating oils to cook your stir-frys.

WOK HEI: COOLING DOWN YOUR WOK 5 WAYS

1) CHANGE THE "HEIGHT OF FIRE"

Pretty obvious, this one! Turn the knob on your gas or ceramic stoves, or press a few buttons on the more modern electric and induction stoves.

2) REMOVE THE WOK FROM DIRECT HEAT

If it's a thin wok, it should cool down within 10 to 15 seconds. Once your dish has cooled enough and is ready for the next ingredient, place your wok back onto the heat again.

3) STIR AND SHAKE

Give your food a good stir with a spoon while shaking your wok back and forth.

4) FOLDING

Using your ladle or spoon to fold in your stir-fry is a great way of cooling your wok down without getting food everywhere. Keep your spoon facing downward and fold from the back into the stir-fry to help the cooling process.

5) FLICK AND TOSS

Learn how to flick and toss your wok properly, giving it a long push forward and a quick flick back. Practice with a small cup of raw rice and you'll soon master it (although a dustpan and brush might be needed after the first few attempts!).

In my opinion, every stir-frying lesson should start with this, the Chinese version of the omelet challenge, that classic test of the French kitchen. This dish is a real test of your control of heat or wok hei (see page 32)—if the wok is not hot enough, the egg will stick to the bottom, while too hot and the food is bound to burn, leaving you with a mountain of speckled rice with bits of crunchy egg in between. Lastly, if you combine your ingredients in the wrong order you'll end up with a rice omelet. No pressure though, right? Still, master this and you'll have picked up some key skills that will serve you well on your Chinese culinary journey.

GARLIC AND EGG-FRIED RICE

SERVES: 2
PREPARATION TIME: 10 MINUTES
COOKING TIME: 5 MINUTES

2 small garlic cloves
3½ oz (100 g) Chinese chives (optional)
1 scallion
1½ cups (250 g) Simply Cooked Jasmine
   Rice (see pages 22 to 23), cooled
1½ Tbsp vegetable
   oil or garlic oil
1 egg
¾ cup (80 g) petit pois

The Sauce
1 to 2 Tbsp light soy sauce
1 tsp sesame oil
Freshly ground black pepper, to taste

PREPARATION

- Finely slice the garlic and mince the Chinese chives. Slice the scallions into rings.

- Put the cooked rice in a small bowl and run a spoon through the grains to separate them as much as possible. (This will help when you add the rice to the dish later.)

✲ **BUILD YOUR WOK CLOCK:** place your egg at 12 o'clock, then arrange the garlic, chives, rice, peas, sauce ingredients, and scallions clockwise around the plate.

COOKING

- Heat 1 Tbsp of vegetable or garlic oil in a wok over high heat until smoking-hot, then crack the egg into the wok. Carefully fold the white of the egg with a spatula so as not to burn it, trying not to break the yolk as you go. Once the egg is halfway cooked and the white is fully opaque, break the yolk and cut into the white with your spatula, creating pieces.

- Now push the egg to one side of the wok to allow space for your rice, add another ½ Tbsp of vegetable oil and bring it to high heat. (You may also remove the egg from the pan if you feel more comfortable or have a small wok and need the space.) Once smoking-hot, add the garlic and Chinese chives, and stir-fry for 10 to 20 seconds.

- Add the rice to the wok, keeping high heat, and mix well, trying to separate the rice grains so as to remove any large clumps. Once the rice is well mixed, add the peas and continue to stir-fry for 1 minute.

- Pour the soy sauce over the rice and stir-fry until the rice has absorbed all the soy sauce and become drier, about 1 minute. Once the grains of rice are "jumping" around the bottom of your wok, the rice is ready. (We call this "dancing rice" in the school.)

- Add the sesame oil and mix together well, then season with black pepper to taste. Spoon into a large bowl and sprinkle over the scallion to finish.

↻ **SWAPSIES:** Can't find Chinese chives? Use garlic shoots, wild garlic, or regular chives instead.

! **TIP:** To make garlic oil at home, take ⅞ cup (200 ml) vegetable oil, place a whole bulb of garlic in it and bring it to low-medium heat in a pan. Simmer for 10 minutes, or until you get an intense garlicky aroma. Transfer to a sealed container and store for up to 3 weeks.

Noodles are a key ingredient in Chinese cooking, and learning how to handle them properly in the wok is essential. The "Tummy and Head" technique (see below) needed to evenly distribute the vegetables among the noodles and keep each strand separate without any "clumping" or breaking is one that many people find difficult to grasp at first, so don't lose hope if it takes time to master. The Hong Kong tradition is to have these for breakfast alongside rice oatmeal and savory doughnuts.

HONG KONG-STYLE FRIED NOODLES

SERVES: 2
PREPARATION TIME: 20 MINUTES
COOKING TIME: 5 MINUTES

3½ oz (100 g) dried egg noodles or chop
  suey-style noodles
1 carrot
5¼ oz (150 g) bok choy
1 cup (100 g) bean sprouts
2 shiitake mushrooms, soaked
  (see page 47)
1 scallion
1½ Tbsp vegetable oil or garlic oil

The Sauce
1½ Tbsp dark soy sauce
1 tsp sesame oil

PREPARATION

• Soak the egg noodles in hot water for 3 to 5 minutes until they have separated, then drain them and let dry on a clean dish towel for 10 minutes.

• Prepare your vegetables: cut your carrot into matchsticks and finely slice your bok choy and bean sprouts. Drain and finely slice the shiitake mushrooms. Slice the scallion into fine matchsticks and put them into a small bowl.

❋ **BUILD YOUR WOK CLOCK:** Place your sliced carrot at 12 o'clock, then arrange the bok choy, mushrooms, bean sprouts, noodles, and sauce ingredients clockwise around the plate.

COOKING

• Heat 1 Tbsp of vegetable or garlic oil in a wok over high heat until smoking-hot. Add the carrots, bok choy, and mushrooms and stir-fry for 1 minute.

• Push the vegetables to the back of your wok, add the bean sprouts, and stir-fry for another 20 to 30 seconds, then empty all the vegetables from the wok back into a large mixing bowl.

• Heat another ½ Tbsp of vegetable oil in the wok on high heat, add the noodles, and stir-fry for 1 minute, then return the vegetables to the wok along with the dark soy sauce. Stir the noodles from the center of the pan outward, while shaking your wok back and forth, until they are evenly colored by the dark soy sauce. (This is what we call the "tummy and head movement" at the School.)

• Add the scallion and sesame oil and give everything one final stir. Serve in a large bowl.

↻ **SWAPSIES:** Can't find bok choy? Try using green cabbage, seasonal kale, or even large spinach leaves instead.

! **TIP:** These noodles must be made with a good-quality Chinese dark soy sauce and should take no longer than 2 to 3 minutes to cook—if you control the heat correctly, the sauce should caramelize well, creating a glazed finish of dark soy and sesame oil rather than noodles swimming in sauce.

This dish may not actually be Singaporean in origin, seemingly drawing on influences and crossovers in cuisine from various regions throughout Asia—it's actually the noodles or "Singapore vermicelli" that give it its name. Singapore noodles are supposed to be dry, yet packed full of flavor. To get this right, follow the directions closely and remember to keep your wok smoking-hot at all times—NEVER, EVER lose your sizzle!

SINGAPORE NOODLES

SERVES: 2
PREPARATION TIME: 20 MINUTES
COOKING TIME: 5 MINUTES

3½ oz (100 g) dried Singapore vermicelli
   noodles
½ onion
½ red bell pepper
1 scallion
6 large raw tiger or king shrimp, peeled
   and deveined (see page 40)
1 egg
A handful of bean sprouts, washed
1 Tbsp vegetable oil

The Spices
1 tsp Madras curry powder
A pinch or two of chili powder (depending
   on how spicy you like it)
1 fresh Thai chili, finely chopped
1 Tbsp water

The Sauce
¼ tsp salt
1 Tbsp light soy sauce
½ tsp dark soy sauce
1 tsp sesame oil

PREPARATION

- Soak the vermicelli noodles in hot water for 3 minutes until they have separated. Drain them and let dry on a clean dish towel for 10 minutes.

- Finely slice the onion, red bell pepper, and scallion. Put the shrimp in a small bowl or ramekin. Mix the spice and sauce ingredients together in separate ramekins or bowls.

✿ **BUILD YOUR WOK CLOCK:** place your egg at 12 o'clock, then arrange the onion, pepper, shrimp, bean sprouts, noodles, spice, and sauce bowls and lastly your scallion clockwise around your plate.

COOKING

- Heat the vegetable oil in a wok over high heat until smoking, then crack the egg into the wok. Carefully fold over the white of the egg with a spatula so as not to burn it, trying not to break the yolk as you go. Once the egg is halfway cooked and the white is fully opaque, break the yolk and cut into the white with your spatula, creating pieces.

- Now push the egg to one side of the wok to allow space for your veg and heat until smoking-hot (you may remove the egg from the pan if you feel more comfortable or have a small wok and need the space).

- Once smoking-hot, add the onions and peppers and stir-fry for 1 minute, then add the shrimp and stir-fry for another 30 to 60 seconds until they are lightly browned.

- Add the bean sprouts to the wok and stir-fry for another 20 to 30 seconds, then add the noodles and stir-fry for 1 minute before stirring in the spice mix and pouring over the sauce. Continue to cook, stirring, until the ingredients are thoroughly combined and the noodles have dried out a little and are just starting to stick to the bottom of the wok. Serve in a large bowl and sprinkle over the scallion to finish.

! **TIP:** If you feel the wok is looking a little dry between the addition of ingredients, push everything to one side with a spatula and add an extra ½ Tbsp of oil to the wok. Let the oil heat until smoking before adding the next ingredient. Note—you should never need more than 2 Tbsp of oil for one stir-fry.

The first time I tried this dish I was up in the Sichuanese highlands, having driven for eight hours before stopping for lunch. I was in search of a cure for my serious "Panger" (similar to the word "hangry"—what we Pangs become when we aren't fed in time) and ordered this as a side to accompany a few other chili broths, though its simple, bold flavors were so good we could easily have had it on its own. Sweet, sour, spicy, and crunchy, this really is irresistibly tasty.

FLASH-FRIED CABBAGE WITH DRIED CHILES AND SWEETENED SOY

SERVES: 4
PREPARATION TIME: 10 MINUTES
COOKING TIME: 5 MINUTES

3 garlic cloves
1 whole sweetheart cabbage
1 medium ripe tomato
5 to 10 large dried red chiles
1 to 2 Tbsp vegetable oil

The Sauce
2 Tbsp rice wine
1 Tbsp Chinkiang black rice vinegar
1 Tbsp light soy sauce
½ Tbsp granulated sugar
¼ tsp dark soy sauce
½ tsp salt

PREPARATION

- Finely slice your garlic cloves, chop your cabbage into large chunks, and cut your tomato into eighths. Combine your sauce ingredients in a small bowl.

- ✳ BUILD YOUR WOK CLOCK: place your chiles at 12 o'clock, then arrange your garlic, tomatoes, cabbage, and lastly your sauce bowl clockwise around your plate.

COOKING

- Heat 1 Tbsp of vegetable or garlic oil in a wok over high heat until smoking-hot.

- Add the dried chiles and garlic to the wok and stir-fry for 30 seconds, then add the tomatoes and cabbage and stir-fry for another 1 minute, keeping the heat high.

- Pour your sauce into the wok, bring to vigorous boil, and stir-fry for another 2 to 3 minutes until the cabbage is tender but still crunchy and the sauce has reduced by a third. Serve.

- ❗ TIP: Beware when cooking this dish the traditional way; the hot oil and chiles will create a lot of smoke! If you want to cook this without such a "smoky" effect, you may add the chiles later in the cooking process; however, the finish may not be 100% the same, as the oil will not take in the essence of the chile.

This is the type of dish that I used to get as an after-school treat when we were kids, but only if my dad was home from work before my mom. Before even entering the kitchen, the aroma coming from the smoking-hot wok would hit us, and I would imagine the cheeky smirk of pride on my dad's face. He was cooking us all a "secret snack." This dish works as a great treat that always hits the spot, or even as a healthy dinner.

STIR-FRIED SHRIMP, EDAMAME, AND PINE NUT LETTUCE WRAPS

SERVES: 2 TO 4 AS PART OF A MEAL
PREPARATION TIME: 20 MINUTES
COOKING TIME: 5 MINUTES

1 iceberg lettuce
10½ oz (300 g) raw shrimp, peeled and
  deveined (see Tip)
½ red bell pepper
1 scallion
2 garlic cloves
5¼ oz (150 g) edamame beans,
  fresh or frozen
3 Tbsp pine nuts
1 Tbsp vegetable oil

The Sauce
1 Tbsp light soy sauce
A dash of sesame oil

The Dressing
6 Tbsp hoisin sauce
3 Tbsp water

PREPARATION

- Remove the stalk of the lettuce by chopping off the bottom third, being careful not to tear any leaves. Turn the trimmed lettuce upside down, place it in the center of a mixing bowl, and pour over hot water very briefly before submerging it in ice-cold water for at least a minute. (This process will help you separate the leaves from each other without effort.) Separate and drain the individual leaves, trimming them for presentation if needed, and place in the refrigerator to cool.

- Butterfly the shrimp, cutting a line from underneath the head of the shrimp to the tip of the tail using a sharp knife and opening up the shrimp fully.

- Finely dice your red bell pepper, finely slice your scallions, and chop your garlic. Mix your sauce and dressing ingredients together in separate bowls or small ramekins.

�֎ **BUILD YOUR WOK CLOCK:** place your butterflied shrimp at 12 o'clock, then arrange the red bell pepper, edamame beans, garlic, pine nuts, scallion, and sauce bowl clockwise around your plate.

COOKING

- Heat the vegetable oil in a wok over high heat until smoking-hot.

- Add the shrimp and stir-fry for 30 seconds, then add the red pepper, edamame beans, and garlic and continue to stir-fry for 1 minute, keeping the heat high.

- Add the pine nuts and stir-fry for 30 seconds, then pour over the sauce and continue to stir-fry until the shrimp are lightly golden brown on the outside.

- Sprinkle over the scallion and transfer to a serving plate or bowl.

- Pile the lettuce leaves on a separate plate and serve with the dressing. Let everyone help themselves by filling a leaf with a spoonful of the shrimp mixture, wrapping it into a bundle, and dipping it into the dressing.

! **TIP:** To devein a shrimp, use a small, sharp knife to make a slit along the middle of the back to expose the dark vein, then pull it out. Alternatively insert a toothpick roughly three-quarters of the way up the back of the shrimp and pull the vein up and out of the shrimp.

When thinking of Hong Kong, most people picture a big, busy, skyscraper-filled city, but I immediately imagine (and can even almost taste) a giant bowl of chile and garlic clams, enjoyed while sitting next to the seafront of Sai Kung harbor. Dotted with fishing boats, Sai Kung is nothing but low-rise houses, beaches, and restaurants full of fresh seafood— quite the contrast to modern Hong Kong. The Chinese like to think that clams look like old gold bullions, and therefore represent good wealth, which is why this dish is eaten a lot during Chinese New Year.

CHILE AND GARLIC "WEALTHY" CLAMS

SERVES: 2 TO 4 WITH SIDE DISHES
PREPARATION TIME: 15 MINUTES
COOKING TIME: 5 MINUTES

1 lb 2 oz (500 g) fresh clams
2 garlic cloves
a thumb-size piece of ginger
2 fresh red chiles
A small handful of fresh cilantro sprigs
1 Tbsp vegetable oil

The Sauce
1 tsp chili bean sauce
4 Tbsp Shaoxing rice wine
4 Tbsp water
1 Tbsp light soy sauce
½ tsp dark soy sauce

PREPARATION

- Sort through the clams, discarding any that don't close when tapped gently.

- Wash the clams thoroughly by running them under cold water and rinsing them 3 or 4 times, then place the clams in a mixing bowl.

- Mince the garlic, ginger, and chiles. Mix the sauce ingredients together in a small bowl or ramekin.

❋ BUILD YOUR WOK CLOCK: place your chopped garlic at 12 o'clock, then arrange the ginger, chiles, clams, sauce bowl, and cilantro clockwise around your plate.

COOKING

- Heat the oil in a wok over medium heat, then add the garlic, chile, and ginger and stir-fry for 20 to 30 seconds until fragrant.

- Increase the heat to high and add the clams to the wok, then immediately pour over the sauce and bring to a vigorous boil. Cover with a lid and cook for 3 to 5 minutes, shaking occasionally, until the clams have opened up. Some clams may still remain closed after cooking—discard any that haven't opened after this time.

- Tip the clams into a large bowl, stir in the cilantro sprigs, and serve.

↺ SWAPSIES: Chili bean sauce is made mainly of minced fermented fava beans, chile, and garlic. If you cannot find it, blend together 3 fresh large red chiles, 2 garlic cloves, and 1 Tbsp of canned lima beans along with 1 Tbsp of the brine solution from the lima beans for a close substitution.

! TIP: As with all seafood, the most important tip here is not to overcook the clams—remember to control the heat of your wok by shaking it when needed, so as to cook them just through, but no more.

If you are looking for a way to spice up that weekly salmon fillet that sits in your freezer begging not to be pan-fried or baked again, then this should give you some inspiration! The sugar snap peas provide a great crunch to the dish, while the XO sauce—a type of chili oil packed full of dried shrimp and scallops—adds a real depth of flavor to this luxurious yet simple midweek meal.

SALMON BITES IN XO ONION SAUCE

SERVES: 4
PREPARATION TIME: 20 MINUTES
COOKING TIME: 10 MINUTES

1 onion
3 garlic cloves
2 large fresh red chiles
A small handful of cilantro
1 lb 2 oz (500 g) salmon fillet, skin off and pinboned (ask your fish supplier to do this for you)
10½ oz (300 g) sugar snap peas
2 Tbsp vegetable oil

The Sauce
4 Tbsp XO sauce
2 Tbsp light soy sauce
1 Tbsp oyster sauce
2 Tbsp sweet chili sauce
⅞ cup (200 ml) chicken or fish broth

PREPARATION

- Finely slice the onion, garlic, and chile. Coarsely chop the cilantro.

- Cut the salmon into ⅜ to ¾-in (1- to 2-cm) bite-size pieces. Mix the sauce ingredients together in a bowl.

- ❋ **BUILD YOUR WOK CLOCK:** place your sliced onion at 12 o'clock, then arrange the garlic, chile, sugar snap peas, salmon, sauce bowl, and cilantro clockwise around your plate.

COOKING

- Heat 1 Tbsp of vegetable oil in a wok over high heat until smoking-hot.

- Add the onion, garlic, and chile and stir-fry for 30 seconds until lightly browned, then add the sugar snap peas and stir-fry for another minute until the peas are slightly colored.

- Transfer the ingredients from the wok to a bowl, add another 1 Tbsp of oil to the wok, and return to smoking point. Let smoke for 5 seconds to ensure the wok is hot enough for the fish to sear well without sticking, then add the salmon. Stir fry for 1 to 2 minutes until the salmon is browned on all sides.

- Return the vegetables to the wok, pour over the sauce, and bring to a vigorous boil. Cook for another 1 minute until the sauce has thickened and reduced enough to just coat the ingredients, then transfer to a large dish. Sprinkle over the cilantro and serve with a side of steamed rice.

- ❗ **TIP:** The best way to turn the salmon (or any fragile ingredient) in the wok while stir-frying without breaking up the delicate pieces is to use a spatula, lifting up and folding the ingredients gently from underneath.

This light and simple recipe will show you just how easy it is to showcase the freshness of good local produce. This dish is best cooked in the springtime during the short asparagus season, when the vegetable is as sweet as it can be and we are starting to think about lighter, fresher flavors.

STIR-FRIED SCALLOPS AND ASPARAGUS IN SHAOXING RICE WINE

SERVES: 2
PREPARATION TIME: 15 MINUTES
COOKING TIME: 5 MINUTES

A bunch of large asparagus
A small piece of ginger
2 garlic cloves
1 scallion
8 king scallops
1 tsp cornstarch
2 Tbsp vegetable oil

The Sauce
1 Tbsp light soy sauce
1 Tbsp oyster sauce
2 Tbsp Shaoxing rice wine
1 tsp sesame oil

PREPARATION

- Snap off and discard the ends of the asparagus, and cut the rest of the stalks diagonally into 1-in (2.5-cm) pieces. Finely slice the ginger, garlic, and scallions.

- Thoroughly wash the scallops under cold running water. Place in a small bowl or ramekin, add the cornstarch and, using your hands, gently massage it into the scallops until well combined.

- Mix the sauce ingredients together in a separate bowl or ramekin.

- ❇ **BUILD YOUR WOK CLOCK:** place your chopped asparagus at 12 o'clock, then arrange the ginger, garlic, scallop bowl, scallion and sauce bowl clockwise around your plate.

COOKING

- Heat 1 Tbsp of vegetable oil in a wok over high heat until smoking-hot.

- Add the ginger and garlic and stir-fry for 30 seconds until slightly softened, then add the asparagus and stir-fry for another 2 minutes until the asparagus is just tender and lightly colored.

- Transfer the ingredients from the wok to a bowl, add another 1 Tbsp of oil to the wok and return to smoking point. Add the scallops and stir-fry for 1 minute, until browned on all sides. Return the vegetables to the wok, pour over the sauce, and bring to a vigorous boil. Cook for another 30 seconds until the sauce is silky-smooth and just beginning to coat the scallops. Transfer to a large dish, sprinkle over the scallion, and serve.

- ↻ **SWAPSIES:** If scallops don't sit on your midweek shopping list, simply swap them out here for shrimp or fresh, firm tofu pieces for something different but just as tasty.

This classic Cantonese combination works either as a lovely accompaniment to any meal or as a substantial main course with a side of rice. The meatiness and varied textures of the different mushrooms give it a great bite and a real depth of flavor. Use whatever type of mushroom you can find in season—they all taste good!

STIR-FRIED BOK CHOY WITH CHINESE MUSHROOM SAUCE

SERVES: 2
PREPARATION TIME: 15 MINUTES PLUS SOAKING
COOKING TIME: 1 HOUR

A thumb-size piece of ginger
5¼ oz (150 g) wild mushrooms, trimmed
10½ oz (300 g) bok choy
6 shiitake mushrooms, soaked, drained, and soaking water set aside (see Tip)
1 tsp sesame oil
2 Tbsp vegetable oil
A pinch of salt
A handful of coarsely chopped cilantro, to garnish

The Sauce
1½ Tbsp vegetarian oyster sauce or oyster sauce
1 Tbsp light soy sauce
2 Tbsp Shaoxing rice wine
½ tsp dark soy sauce
½ tsp granulated sugar

PREPARATION

- Finely slice the ginger and chop the fresh mushrooms into chunks. Slice the bok choy lengthwise into quarters.

- Mix the sauce ingredients together in a ramekin or small bowl. Pour 1¼ cups (300 ml) of the reserved mushroom soaking water into a separate bowl.

❀ **BUILD YOUR WOK CLOCK:** place the sliced ginger at 12 o'clock, then arrange the soaked mushrooms, sauce bowl, mushroom soaking water, fresh mushrooms, sesame oil, and bok choy clockwise around your plate.

COOKING

- Heat 1 Tbsp of oil in a heavy saucepan or clay pot over medium heat, add half the ginger and the soaked mushrooms to the pan, and fry for 2 to 3 minutes until the ginger has softened and is fragrant. Pour over the sauce and bring to a vigorous boil, then add the mushroom soaking water, bring to a simmer, and cook for 40 minutes, or until the sauce has reduced by half.

- Five minutes before the mushroom sauce is ready, heat a wok over medium-high heat, add the wild mushrooms, and flash-fry for 1 minute until the mushrooms are lightly browned on the edges. Tip the mushrooms into the sauce and let simmer.

- Return the wok to heat, add the remaining 1 Tbsp of vegetable oil and heat until smoking-hot. Add the remaining ginger and stir-fry for 20 seconds, then add the bok choy and stir-fry for 1 minute.

- Add 2 Tbsp of water, season the bok choy with a pinch of salt, drizzle over the sesame oil, and cover with a lid. Cook for another 1 to 2 minutes until the bok choy leaves are wilted but the stalks still retain their vibrant green color.

- Remove the pan from the heat and arrange the bok choy in layers on a large serving plate. Pour over the mushroom sauce and garnish with a little cilantro.

❗ **TIP:** To rehydrate dried mushrooms, cover them in (300ml) hot water and let soak for at least 1 hour (preferably overnight). Drain them before using, setting aside the soaking water for use in your recipe, if necessary.

↻ **SWAPSIES:** While wild mushrooms give this dish a nice mix of textures and flavors, if you can't find them regular white mushrooms will work fine.

The region of Sichuan is situated on the Western side of China and is therefore heavily influenced by ingredients from Tibet and northern India—the most significant of which, Sichuan peppercorns, has become increasingly popular in the West in recent years. Sichuan peppercorns (dried red berries, native to China) have a distinct fragrance when crushed and provide a unique numbing feeling all over the tongue: something the Chinese call ma la. They can be easily found in most Asian grocery stores.

SCHOOL OF WOK'S STIR-FRIED SICHUAN CHICKEN

SERVES: 4
PREPARATION TIME: 20 MINUTES
COOKING TIME: 15 MINUTES

½ onion
1 red bell pepper
14 oz (400 g) boneless chicken thighs
3 garlic cloves
1 Thai chile
1 scallion
2 tsp Sichuan peppercorns
10 dried red chiles
1⅓ cups (200 g) cashews
1½ Tbsp vegetable oil

The Marinade
1 tsp sesame oil
2 tsp granulated sugar
A large pinch of Chinese five-spice
3 Tbsp light soy sauce
1½ Tbsp cornstarch

The Sauce
2 tsp chili paste or chili bean paste
2 Tbsp light soy sauce
2 Tbsp hoisin sauce
3 Tbsp rice wine

PREPARATION

- Slice the onion and red bell pepper into fine matchsticks and the chicken into 1¼-in (3-cm) wide strips. Put the chicken into a small mixing bowl, add the marinade ingredients and, using your hands, massage the pieces until they are evenly coated.

- Mince the garlic and Thai chile, and finely slice your scallion. Crush the Sichuan peppercorns with a mortar and pestle. Mix all the sauce ingredients together in a small bowl or ramekin.

- ✿ BUILD YOUR WOK CLOCK: place your sliced onion at 12 o'clock, then arrange the bell peppers, dried chiles, chicken bowl, crushed peppercorns, garlic, Thai chile, sauce bowl, cashews, and scallions clockwise around your plate.

COOKING

- Heat 1 Tbsp of vegetable oil in a wok over high heat until smoking-hot. Add the onions, red bell peppers, and dried red chiles and stir-fry for 1 to 2 minutes until the onions are lightly browned and slightly softened.

- Reduce the heat to medium (so as not to burn the onions), push the veg to the side of the wok, and add ½ Tbsp of vegetable oil to the center.

- Bring the wok to smoking point, add the chicken, and stir-fry 3 to 5 minutes until golden brown on all sides.

- Lower the heat to medium, add the crushed peppercorns and garlic to the wok, and stir-fry for another 2 minutes, then add the Thai chile and sauce and continue to stir-fry over medium-high heat for another 2 minutes, or until the sauce has thickened and reduced and is sticking to the chicken.

- Add the cashews and cook for a final 30 to 60 seconds, tossing the wok to combine all the ingredients well. Tip onto a large plate and sprinkle over the scallion to finish. Serve.

- ↻ SWAPSIES: Can't find Sichuan peppercorns? Swap them out with a mix of crushed juniper berries and chili flakes.

- ! TIP: If you're a keen chile eater and fancy something with a little more punch then throw in a mixture of different types of chiles here: dried or fresh, whatever you can get your hands on.

The literal translation of this dish, "old pocked woman tofu," may not sound particularly appetizing, but stick with it, as the result is a lovely, spicy, brothlike dish that highlights how good tofu is at absorbing flavor. Served with a bowl of rice on the side it's the ultimate winter one-wok-wonder.

MA PO TOFU

SERVES: 4
PREPARATION TIME: 30 MINUTES
COOKING TIME: 10 MINUTES

1 small onion
2 garlic cloves
2 fresh Thai chiles
A small handful of cilantro
10½ oz (300 g) firm silken tofu (fresh or packaged tofu are both fine to use)
2 tsp preserved black beans
1½ tsp Sichuan peppercorns
14 oz (400 g) ground pork
2 Tbsp Chiu Chow chili oil (the oil from the top of the pot only)

The Marinade
2 tsp sesame oil
A pinch of granulated sugar
1 Tbsp light soy sauce

The Sauce
2 tsp chili bean paste or hot chili paste
2 Tbsp light soy sauce
3 Tbsp rice wine
1 ⅔ cups (400 ml) chicken broth

PREPARATION

- Dice the onion. Mince the garlic, Thai chiles, and cilantro. Cut the silken tofu into ¾-in (2-cm) cubes.

- Wash and drain the preserved black beans, place them in a sealable plastic bag with the Sichuan peppercorns, and bash them with a rolling pin until lightly crushed.

- Place the meat in a bowl, add the marinade ingredients, and massage together with your hands. Mix the sauce ingredients together in a separate bowl.

✿ BUILD YOUR WOK CLOCK: place your diced onion at 12 o'clock, then arrange the garlic, chile, crushed black beans and peppercorns, meat bowl, sauce bowl, tofu cubes, and cilantro clockwise around your plate.

COOKING

- Heat the Chiu Chow chili oil in a wok over medium-high heat until smoking-hot.

- Add the onion to the pan and stir-fry for 1 minute until the onions are lightly browned and starting to soften. Add the garlic, black bean and peppercorn mix, and chile to the pan, followed immediately by the marinated pork. Stir-fry for another 2 minutes until the ground pork is separated and browned, then pour over the sauce and bring to a vigorous boil.

- Add the diced tofu to the wok, reduce the heat to medium, and simmer for 5 minutes, stirring gently so as not to break up the tofu pieces too much. Continue to bubble away until the sauce has thickened and reduced by a third but the dish is still nice and brothy. Remove from the heat.

- Serve in a large bowl and sprinkle over the finely chopped cilantro to garnish.

🍃 SWAPSIES: To make this dish completely vegetarian, swap out the ground pork for finely chopped soaked shiitake mushrooms.

❗ TIP: If your sauce isn't thickening up properly, mix together ½ Tbsp of cornstarch with 2 Tbsp of cold water and stir it into your sauce before folding in the tofu. Alternatively, if you happen to overboil your sauce, just add a little hot water to thin it out.

All regions of China, and in fact many cuisines of the world have their own distinct sweet-and-sour combinations. When School of Wok started in 2009, the first thing that anyone wanted to learn was how to make a classic sweet-and-sour chicken. Although I have nothing against a good homecooked Cantonese-style sweet-and-sour, as time has gone on our customers have moved on to develop an interest in what an "authentic sweet-and-sour" might taste like. This dish—essentially the sweet-and-sour flavor that Sichuan is famous for—has also made its mark across the world, alongside the Cantonese sweet-and-sour chicken ball, of course.

SWEET-AND-SOUR PORK STRIPS

SERVES: 4
PREPARATION TIME: 30 MINUTES
COOKING TIME: 10 MINUTES

½ red onion
3½ oz (100 g) bamboo shoots
3 Tbsp pickled cabbage or
    pickled bok choy
1 scallion
3 garlic cloves
A thumb-size piece of ginger
2¼ oz (60 g) cloud ear fungus, soaked
    and drained (see page 47)
1½ tsp Sichuan peppercorns
10½ oz (300 g) pork blade steak or loin
2 tsp chili bean paste
1 to 2 Tbsp vegetable oil

The Marinade
1 tsp granulated sugar
1½ Tbsp light soy sauce
2 Tbsp Shaoxing rice wine
1½ tsp sesame oil
1 Tbsp cornstarch

The Sauce
1 Tbsp granulated sugar
1 to 2 tsp Chiu Chow chili oil
1 Tbsp Chinkiang black rice vinegar
1 Tbsp hoisin sauce
2 Tbsp chicken broth
1 tsp dark soy sauce

PREPARATION
- Finely slice the onion, bamboo shoots, pickled cabbage, and scallion. Mince the garlic and slice the ginger into matchsticks. Shred the drained cloud ear fungus (if not already shredded) and lightly crush the Sichuan peppercorns.

- Bash the pork well with the side of the cleaver, and then half-grind it using a rocking motion (see page 16 —this will not only help tenderize the meat, but it will also help to get all the marinade and sauce ingredients to soak into the meat itself). Slice the meat into thin strips, put it in a bowl, and cover with the marinade ingredients, massaging them into the meat well with your hands.

- Mix the sauce ingredients together well in a small bowl or ramekin.

✿ BUILD YOUR WOK CLOCK: place your sliced onion at 12 o'clock, then arrange the bamboo shoots, pork bowl, ginger, garlic, peppercorns, chili paste, shredded fungus, pickled vegetables, sauce bowl, and scallion clockwise around your plate.

COOKING
- Heat the vegetable oil in a wok over high heat until smoking-hot.

- Add the onion and bamboo shoots and stir-fry for 1 minute, then add the pork slices and stir-fry, keeping the heat high, for another minute until golden brown.

- Add the ginger, garlic, Sichuan peppercorns, and chili paste and stir-fry for another 30 seconds, then add the shredded fungus and pickled vegetables and stir-fry for another 1 minute. Pour over the sauce, bring to a vigorous boil, and cook, stirring, for 1 to 2 minutes until the sauce has slightly thickened and reduced to a coating consistency.

- Transfer to a serving plate or bowl and sprinkle over the scallion slices to finish. Serve.

↻ SWAPSIES: Chinkiang black rice vinegar has a unique savory-sweet aroma that comes from the fermented husks of black rice. If you cannot find it, try mixing together 3 Tbsp of thin balsamic vinegar with 1 Tbsp of light soy sauce and 1 tsp of sugar instead.

Black bean sauce is really not hard to make, but for some reason it tends to be too overpowering or gelatinous in most restaurants and takeouts. Thanks to my Aunty Eunice, I learned an incredibly handy tip that you can use in so many dishes … and even maybe in life (we were making lobster noodles at the time): "Get it drunk first and it'll all be OK." Here the addition of a fine lager or light beer to the black bean sauce really lightens it up and brings out the flavors of the black beans and ginger.

STIR-FRIED BLACK BEAN BEEF IN BEER

SERVES: 4
PREPARATION TIME: 20 MINUTES
COOKING TIME: 5 MINUTES

1 onion
1 green or red bell pepper
A thumb-size piece of ginger
1 scallion
3 garlic cloves
1 Tbsp preserved salted black beans,
   rinsed and drained in cold water
a pinch of salt
14 oz (400 g) sirloin or rib-eye steak
2 Tbsp vegetable oil
A dash of sesame oil

The Marinade
½ Tbsp sesame oil
2 tsp granulated sugar
½ tsp Chinese five-spice
2 Tbsp light soy sauce
2 Tbsp Shaoxing rice wine
1½ Tbsp cornstarch

The Sauce
2 Tbsp oyster sauce
¼ tsp dark soy sauce
⅞ cup (200 ml) lager

PREPARATION

- Finely slice the onion, pepper, ginger, and scallion. Mince the garlic and place in a small bowl or ramekin with the preserved black beans and salt, lightly crushing the beans and garlic together with the back of a spoon to release their flavors.

- Finely slice the meat, place it in a mixing bowl, and add all the marinade ingredients except the cornstarch. Using your hands, massage the ingredients into the meat until it is well coated, then add the cornstarch, and repeat until everything is well combined.

- Mix the sauce ingredients together in a bowl.

✳ **BUILD YOUR WOK CLOCK:** place your sliced onion at 12 o'clock, then arrange the peppers, ginger, garlic, and black bean mixture, beef bowl, sauce bowl, and scallion clockwise around your plate.

COOKING

- Heat 1 Tbsp of vegetable oil in a wok over high heat until smoking-hot. Add the onion and peppers, reduce the heat to medium, and stir-fry for 1 minute, or until the onion has slightly softened. Transfer the onions and peppers to a bowl.

- Add another 1 Tbsp of oil to the wok and return to smoking point. Let smoke for 5 seconds (to ensure the wok is hot enough for the meat to sear well without sticking), then add the ginger, garlic, and black bean mixture and beef to the wok. Spread the meat out across the bottom of the wok in one layer using a wooden spoon or spatula and let sear for 30 seconds until browned, then turn and repeat on the other side.

- Once the meat has browned on both sides, return the vegetables to the wok and pour over the sauce. Bring to a vigorous boil and stir-fry for 2 to 3 minutes until the sauce has thickened and reduced slightly. Stir in the sesame oil, spoon onto a serving plate, and sprinkle over the scallion to finish.

↻ **SWAPSIES:** If you don't fancy using beer (or any other alcohol) here, the lager can be replaced with any chicken or vegetable broth—even a light, sharp lemonade or club soda would work well.

Although I have managed to convince my previously vegetarian wife to eat pork belly, duck, lamb, and frog's legs (all in in less than a week I might add —I'm persuasive!), as her family are from a Hindu background, beef is something that I will never be able to share with her. So, with her in mind, I created this dish as an alternative to a stir-fried beef. Venison steaks stay tender when flash-fried in a wok, while the sourness of the tamarind and sweetness from the kecap manis give this dish a Malaysian-Chinese feel.

FLASH-FRIED VENISON AND BROCCOLI WITH GINGER AND SCALLION

SERVES: 2
PREPARATION TIME: 15 MINUTES PLUS MARINATING
COOKING TIME: 5 MINUTES

A thumb-size piece of ginger
2 scallions
5 to 10 stems of tenderstem broccoli
  or kai lan
7 to 10½ oz (200 to 300 g) venison steaks
A handful of deep-fried shallots (optional)
1½ Tbsp vegetable oil

The Marinade
1 Tbsp light soy sauce
2 Tbsp Shaoxing rice wine
1 tsp sesame oil
½ Tbsp cornstarch

The Sauce
2 Tbsp tamarind concentrate
1 Tbsp hoisin sauce
1 Tbsp kecap manis
  (sweet soy sauce)
3½ Tbsp (50 ml) chicken broth

PREPARATION

- Slice the ginger and scallions into fine matchsticks. Chop the broccoli or kai lan stems into thirds, then blanch them in boiling water for 2 minutes. Drain and set aside.

- Slice the venison steaks into large ⅜- to ¾-in (1- to 2-cm) chunks, put them in a bowl, and add all the marinade ingredients except the cornstarch. Using your hands, massage the ingredients into the meat until they are coated, then add the cornstarch and repeat until everything is well combined. For best results, let the meat marinate overnight in the refrigerator.

- Mix the sauce ingredients together in a small bowl or ramekin.

✿ BUILD YOUR WOK CLOCK: place your sliced ginger at 12 o'clock, then arrange the scallions, venison, broccoli, sauce bowl, and deep-fried shallots, if using, clockwise around your plate.

COOKING

- Heat 1 Tbsp of vegetable oil in a wok over high heat until smoking-hot. Add the ginger and half the scallions and stir-fry for 1 minute until the scallions have softened.

- Push the ingredients to the side of the wok, add the remaining ½ Tbsp of oil to the center, and return to smoking point. Add the venison, cover with the ginger and scallions, and stir-fry for 1 minute.

- Add the broccoli, pour over the sauce, and bring to a vigorous boil. Cook, stirring, for another 30 seconds, then spoon into a serving bowl. Sprinkle over the remaining scallion and the deep-fried shallots, if using, and serve.

❗ TIP: Tamarind lends a dish its natural sour flavor and can be found in various forms: in its pods, with its seeds in a block of paste, or as a strained concentrate. If you use it a lot I recommend you buy the paste and thin it down with water yourself at home.

DEEP-FRYING

While deep-frying may not necessarily be the healthiest of cooking processes, there is something incredibly delicious about the unique texture that it creates. In Chinese cooking, deep-fried dishes definitely have a place in the "balancing puzzle." Not only do they create added texture within a meal, but deep-frying also seems to engage a different sense of savory flavor on our palates, which is why I think something deep-fried is so moreish. It is important to see this chapter as that segment of a balancing act when pieced together with a whole family meal, rather than dishes that should sit alone on the dinner table every night of the week.

The Chinese tend to use deep-frying in a variety of situations. From an instant cooking process for quick appetizers, finger foods, and pastries to creating an immediate seal for dishes that require that added crispiness or crunch. Deep-fried batters can also help to wrap tasty sauces and intense flavors around a food item, bringing several components of a dish together; such as in sweet-and-sour chicken or tofu. Within this deep-frying chapter you will come across different pastries as well as both wet and dry batters, which will form different crispy layers around your food, showcasing a variety of deep-frying techniques and outcomes.

Deep-frying is such a big part of Chinese cooking, but it definitely falls into the more adventurous side of home cooking! Here are some handy tips on how to deep-fry in the home kitchen safely as well as successfully.

! TIP: Deep-frying is essentially a sealing process—a great way of locking in the moisture and flavor of whatever you are cooking. When deep-frying correctly, your ingredients should be immersed in enough hot oil to create an immediate seal around the ingredient. As long as the heat of your oil is between 320 to 350°F (160 to 180°C), the ingredients will immediately start to "blister" around the edges, creating that seal that you are looking for.

DEEP-FRYING: THE RULES

1. First and foremost, when deep-frying anything, try not to do anything else at the same time. **No multitasking!**

2. Use a thick, large saucepan or wok. This will ensure the heat is easier to control without warming too quickly, as well as keeping the oil from spitting over the side.

3. Never fill the oil more than halfway up the pan.

4. Bring your high-heating oil (vegetable, sunflower, corn, peanut, canola, or rice bran oil) gradually to heat over medium-high flame.

5. Test the temperature of the oil the Chinese way by dipping a wooden implement (wooden chopstick, bamboo skewer, or the end of a wooden spoon) into the hot oil and resting it carefully in the liquid. At around 284°F (140°C), the wood will start to bubble slowly, however the oil will not be hot enough to deep-fry yet. At around 338 to 350°F (170 to 180°C) the wood will fizz, which would suggest that you are at roughly the right temperature to deep-fry.

6. **NEVER** allow your oil to get so hot that it starts to smoke. If you do see it smoking, it is best to switch the stove off and let it cool for at least 10 minutes before starting again. Unlike when stir-frying, if you allow such a large volume of oil to smoke in a pan or wok the immense heat that is created within that volume of oil will soon turn into flame, which is where deep-frying can become dangerous.

7. Always have a slotted spoon or frying basket and tongs and a mixing bowl covered with two or three sheets of paper towel at the ready to strain off any excess oil from the deep-frying process.

Most Chinese dumplings can either be deep-fried, pan-fried, steamed, or blanched, though there is something incredibly moreish about deep-fried ones with their crunchy exterior and hot, steamy filling. Much like fresh pasta, when made from scratch, dumplings should not be overcooked—whichever way you choose to cook them, the cooking process itself should not take any longer than 5 minutes. The goal is to cook the dough and filling through, while keeping that "al dente" bite. Served with noodles, these make a great alternative to a Sunday lunch.

SHIITAKE AND CHIVE DUMPLINGS

SERVES: 6 (MAKES 20 TO 25 DUMPLINGS)
PREPARATION TIME: 1 HOUR
COOKING TIME: 10 MINUTES

2 cups (225 g) all-purpose flour
½ to ⅝ cup (130 to 150 ml) hot water
vegetable oil, for frying

The Filling
1¾ oz (50 g) rice vermicelli noodles
a handful of cilantro
1 scallion
A thumb-size piece of ginger
1 garlic clove
5 shiitake mushrooms, soaked
  (see page 47) and drained
7 oz (200 g) Chinese chives
5 bok choy leaves
1 leaf of Napa cabbage

The Marinade
1 Tbsp light soy sauce
¼ tsp black pepper
¼ tsp granulated sugar
2 tsp sesame oil
½ Tbsp cornstarch

The Dipping Sauce
4 Tbsp light soy sauce
4 Tbsp Chinkiang black
  rice vinegar
A thumb-size piece of ginger,
  finely sliced

PREPARATION

- Sift the flour into a bowl. Gradually add the water, mixing with a fork to form a dough, then knead it on a lightly dusted counter for 5 minutes until slightly elastic.

- Roll out the dough to a thickness of ¹⁄₃₂ to ¹⁄₁₆ in (1 to 2 mm), then use a 2¾-in (70-mm) diameter circular cutter to cut out as many circles as possible. Set the circles aside on a baking sheet or tray and cover with a dish towel until needed.

- For the filling, put the noodles in a bowl, cover with hot water, and soak for 3 minutes. Drain and dry the noodles on a clean paper towel, then mince them along with all the other filling ingredients. Put the chopped filling ingredients in a bowl along with the marinade ingredients and mix together well.

- Combine the dipping sauce ingredients in a small bowl or ramekin and wrap the dumplings as shown below.

COOKING

- Half-fill a large pot, wok, or deep-fryer with vegetable oil and heat to 350°F (180°C), or until the tip of a wooden chopstick or skewer starts to fizz after a second or so in the oil.

- Carefully add the dumplings in batches of no more than 10 and deep-fry for 3 minutes, until golden brown. Remove the dumplings carefully with a slotted spoon and drain on a plate covered with paper towel. Serve immediately with the dipping sauce.

WRAPPING

1. Place 1 tsp of the filling in the center of each circle of dough. Fold the bottom center over the filling to form a semicircle and pinch the top tight.

2. Pinch the two corners of the semicircle together leaving two symmetrical "Mickey Mouse ear" shapes between your center fold and the corner folds.

3. Now pinch the "ears" in toward you to make four layered folds.

4. Tidy up to create a "half-moon" shape and arrange on a plate.

Spring roll wrappers can be found in all Asian grocery stores and, surprisingly to some, in many Indian grocery stores as well, as they are used across the subcontinent for samosas and other deep-fried snacks. They have a unique elastic texture to them—this comes from the cooking process, where a thin batter is pasted onto giant heated metal rollers and slowly cooked while being rolled out at the same time. Although quite delicate, they are definitely thicker and more pliable than phyllo dough.

HOISIN DUCK SPRING ROLLS

SERVES: 8 TO 10
PREPARATION TIME: 1 HOUR
COOKING TIME: 15 MINUTES

1 pack spring roll wrappers
1 banana, for sticking
Vegetable oil, for frying

The Filling
½ tsp salt
10½ oz (300 g) duck breast
1 leaf of Napa cabbage, finely sliced
½ onion, finely sliced
a handful of cilantro, finely sliced
2 scallions, finely sliced
1 red bell pepper, finely diced
1 Tbsp hoisin sauce

The Marinade
1 Tbsp oyster sauce or vegetarian
  oyster sauce
½ Tbsp light soy sauce
1 Tbsp sweet chili sauce
1 tsp sesame oil
1 Tbsp hoisin sauce
½ tsp dark soy sauce

PREPARATION

- Carefully separate each sheet of spring roll dough and pile up on a plate. Cover the pile with plastic wrap so as not to let the dough dry out.

- For the filling, rub the salt onto the skin of the duck breast and place in a frying pan skin-side down. Bring the pan to medium–high heat and cook off without any oil (plenty of fat will start to render off the duck skin) for 6 minutes, then turn and fry for 5 minutes more. Set aside to cool, then finely chop and mix together with the rest of the filling ingredients and the marinade in a mixing bowl. Wrap the spring rolls as shown below.

COOKING

- Half-fill a large pot, wok, or deep-fryer with vegetable oil and heat to 338°F (170°C), or until the tip of a wooden chopstick or skewer starts to fizz after 2 to 3 seconds in the oil. Carefully add the spring rolls in batches of no more than 10 at a time and deep-fry for 4 minutes until golden brown. Remove the spring rolls carefully with a slotted spoon and drain well on a plate covered with paper towels.

- Serve immediately, accompanied by sweet chili sauce or the homemade chili sauce on page 90.

! **TIP:** The beauty with snacks like spring rolls is that you can put pretty much whatever you like inside them. For a vegetarian spring roll, omit the duck and hoisin sauce and add bean sprouts along with your favorite veg, cut into matchsticks.

WRAPPING

1. Cut open the banana and use it as an edible "glue stick" to mark around the borders. Place the cooled filling in the center of each piece of pastry.

2. Fold over diagonally and stick together, holding your fingertips over the "roll" and using your thumbs to roll the pastry slightly to enclose the filling.

3. Fold the sides and stick them together with the banana.

4. Roll up the pastry and stick the seam together with the banana to close.

I've been trying, testing, and tweaking this recipe since my university days—endless hours of deep-frying bits of squid of all shapes and sizes in different batters. I've tried making it with egg, without egg, with different flours, in different oils, and yet I ALWAYS come back to the simplest option: no egg, just plenty of seasoned cornstarch or potato starch and a clean vat of high-heating oil. The oil must be nice and clean to ensure you get a good golden-brown finish, which is especially important for something as waxy and delicate as squid.

SALT AND PEPPER CHILI SQUID

SERVES: 2 TO 4
PREPARATION TIME: 30 MINUTES
COOKING TIME: 10 MINUTES

1 lb 2 oz (500 g) baby squid, cleaned and
  quills removed (get your fish supplier to
  do this for you)
1⅔ cups (200 g) cornstarch, seasoned with
  ½ tsp salt and ½ tsp pepper
3 garlic cloves
1 fresh red chile (or 1 Thai chile if you like
  it hot)
2 scallions, finely sliced
vegetable oil, for frying
¼ tsp salt
½ tsp black pepper

PREPARATION

- Wash the squid tubes and slice them open to lay them flat. Run the tip of your knife along the squid pieces in a diagonal crisscross pattern (this will help the squid curl up nicely when cooking).

- Place the squid tubes and tentacles in a mixing bowl and cover with the cornstarch, then cover the bowl with a plate or lid. Hold the bowl and lid together firmly and shake to mix well.

- After shaking, use your fingers to massage the cornstarch into the squid until each piece is separate and is as dry as possible. Add more cornstarch if necessary.

- Mince the garlic and chiles. Finely slice the scallions.

✳ **BUILD YOUR WOK CLOCK:** place your squid bowl at 12 o'clock, then arrange the garlic, chile, salt, pepper, and scallions clockwise around your plate.

COOKING

- Half-fill a large pot, wok, or deep-fryer with vegetable oil and heat to 350°F (180°C), or until the tip of a wooden chopstick or skewer starts to fizz after a second or so in the oil.

- Carefully add the squid pieces and deep-fry for 2 to 3 minutes, or until golden brown. Remove the squid pieces carefully with a slotted spoon and drain well on a plate covered with paper towels.

- In a separate wok, heat 1 Tbsp of vegetable oil over medium-high heat. Add the garlic, chile, salt, and pepper, then add the squid and toss together a few times. Transfer to a serving plate and sprinkle over the scallion to finish. Serve immediately.

❗ **TIP:** Make sure you add the squid to the wok immediately as the chiles will kick up a lot of smoke in the pan if you hang around!

While it might not be a totally authentic Chinese dish, shrimp toast does embrace the Chinese culinary ethos of utilizing everything we have access to, and creating as little waste as possible. Around the corner from where my wife and I live in London there is a little French deli that sells the best fresh baguettes around (the type that go stale within 24 hours). I find these to be perfect for making a thicker, more rustic version of the classic shrimp toast.

RUSTIC SHRIMP TOAST

SERVES: 2 TO 4 AS PART OF A MEAL
PREPARATION TIME: 30 MINUTES
COOKING TIME: 5 MINUTES

2 garlic cloves
1 scallion
A handful of cilantro
20 large shrimp, peeled and deveined (see page 40)
Sea salt and freshly ground black pepper
2 tsp sesame oil
1 egg white
1 Tbsp cornstarch
½ stick of stale French baguette
2 tsp sesame seeds
Vegetable oil, for frying

PREPARATION

• Mince the garlic, scallion, cilantro, and shrimp and place in a mixing bowl. Season with salt and pepper, add the sesame oil, egg white, and cornstarch, and beat together with a wooden spoon.

• Slice the baguette in half lengthwise and hollow out the bread, leaving the crust but reserving the soft inside. Finely dice the removed inside of the bread and add to the shrimp mix.

• Spoon the shrimp mix into the hollowed out crust halves, then slice into 1½-in (4-cm) pieces. Sprinkle the sesame seeds over the top of each piece of bread.

COOKING

• Half-fill a large pot, wok, or deep-fryer with vegetable oil and heat to 350°F (180°C), or until the tip of a wooden chopstick or skewer starts to fizz after a second or so in the oil.

• Carefully add the toast slices shrimp-side down and deep-fry for 2 to 3 minutes then turn over and fry for another 1 to 2 minutes until crispy and golden. Remove the pieces carefully with a slotted spoon and drain well on a plate covered with paper towels. Serve immediately with sweet chili dipping sauce on the side.

! TIP: When frying the pieces of shrimp toast, ensure you fry them shrimp-side down first and keep a slotted spoon nearby to ensure they do not turn over. Always keep your plate and paper towel close as the cooking process is relatively fast and requires careful watching.

I've eaten many a fishcake in my life and in a lot of restaurants I find them to be squidgy and rubbery, with the fish almost unidentifiable. This recipe has developed over time, with the base ingredients (excluding the panko bread crumbs) borrowed from a Thai-style spiced fish cake. The ingredients are then mixed with salted egg white for a little classic Chinese flavor, with the minced green beans bringing some added crunch. I like to shape these into golf-ball-size bites so that there is enough fish cake to actually bite into and enjoy the varied textures.

SALTED EGG FISH CAKES

SERVES: 2 TO 4 AS AN APPETIZER
PREPARATION TIME: 40 MINUTES
COOKING TIME: 10 MINUTES

1 oz (25 g) green beans
½ bunch of cilantro
1 egg, beaten
2½ cups + 2 Tbsp (315 g) cornstarch
2¼ cups (300 g) panko bread crumbs
Sea salt and freshly ground black pepper
2 salted eggs or leftover salted egg whites
  (see page 67)
1 x 1¾ oz (50 g) white fish fillet
1 x 2¾ oz (75 g) squid, cleaned and quills
  removed (get your fish supplier to do
  this for you)
1¾ oz (50 g) shrimp, peeled and deveined
  (see page 40)
1 tsp sesame oil
Vegetable oil, for frying

PREPARATION

- Finely chop the beans and coarsely chop the cilantro. Arrange the beaten egg, 2½ cups (300 g) of the cornstarch, and the bread crumbs in separate bowls ready for coating the fish cakes. Season the cornstarch with a little salt and pepper and mix together well.

- If using whole salted eggs, steam them for 10 minutes in a wok with a steamer stand. Once cool, peel off the shells and separate the whites from the yolks, setting aside the yolks for another recipe such as Salted Egg Shrimp (see page 67).

- Slice the white fish fillet, squid, and shrimp into 1¼-in (3-cm) chunks. Keep the squid tentacles separate. Pat the fish and squid dry with paper towel.

- Add the shrimp, fish, salted egg white, and chopped squid tubes to a food processor and blend together to form a smooth paste. Add the tentacles and sesame oil and blend together to combine, then spoon the mixture into a large mixing bowl.

- Add the green beans, cilantro, and the remaining 1 Tbsp of the cornstarch to the fishcake mixture and mix together well. Using your hands, take a golf-ball-size piece of the mix, then roll it in the seasoned cornstarch, then the beaten egg and finally the panko bread crumbs. Repeat with the remaining mix.

COOKING

- Half-fill a large pot, wok, or deep-fryer with vegetable oil and heat to 350°F (180°C), or until the tip of a wooden chopstick or skewer starts to fizz after a second or so in the oil.

- Carefully add half the fish cakes and deep-fry until golden brown, about 4 to 5 minutes. Remove the pieces carefully with a slotted spoon and drain well on a plate covered with paper towels, then transfer to a low oven to keep warm until the second batch is ready. Repeat with the remaining fish cakes and serve immediately.

! TIP: These fish cakes are wonderful served with chili sauce. For a rather special version, try mixing 3 Tbsp of sweet chili sauce with the juice of ½ a lime, 1 clove of minced garlic, and 1 stalk of minced fresh lemongrass.

Salted duck eggs are strange but wonderful ingredients. Generally preserved in either a brine solution or packed densely in charcoal, the eggs have a salted, slightly chalky feel and a very bright yolk. Because of their extreme salty taste and texture, the eggs tend not eaten by themselves, but rather used for making unique sauces or serving alongside roast meats and rice or congee. In this recipe the salted duck egg yolks are used to both thicken and flavor the wrapping sauce for the crispy shrimp.

SALTED EGG SHRIMP

SERVES: 2
PREPARATION TIME: 30 MINUTES PLUS MARINATING
COOKING TIME: 10 MINUTES

10½ oz (300 g) raw king shrimp, peeled
  and deveined (see page 40)
1 Thai chile (optional)
1⅔ cups (200 g) cornstarch
6 fresh curry leaves
Vegetable oil, for frying

The Marinade
½ Tbsp oyster sauce
1 tsp granulated sugar
1 tsp black pepper
½ Tbsp light soy sauce
1 egg white

The Sauce
2 salted eggs
6 Tbsp evaporated milk
2 tsp granulated sugar
A pinch of salt

PREPARATION

- Put the marinade ingredients in a bowl and mix together well, then add the shrimp and let marinate for a minimum of 10 minutes, or up to 2 hours for best results.

- To make the sauce, steam the eggs in a wok with a steamer stand for 10 minutes, then let cool. Once cool, peel off the shells and separate the whites from the yolks. Set aside the whites for use in another recipe (see Tip) and crumble the yolks into a small bowl. Using the underside of a spoon, blend the egg yolk into a paste, then mix it together with the rest of the sauce ingredients until smooth and free of lumps.

- Mince the chile, if using, and set aside.

- Add the cornstarch to the marinated shrimp and mix together with your hands until the shrimp are dry and dusty-white in color.

✱ **BUILD YOUR WOK CLOCK:** put your shrimp at 12 o'clock, then arrange the curry leaves, chile, and sauce bowl clockwise around your plate.

METHOD

- Half-fill a large pot, wok, or deep-fryer with vegetable oil and heat to 350°F (180°C), or until the tip of a wooden chopstick or skewer starts to fizz after a second or so in the oil.

- Carefully add the shrimp and deep-fry until golden brown, about 3 minutes. Remove the shrimp carefully with a slotted spoon and drain well on a plate covered with paper towels.

- In a separate wok, heat ½ Tbsp of vegetable oil over low heat, add the curry leaves and chile, if using, and stir-fry for 30 seconds or so until fragrant. Pour over the sauce and continue to cook, stirring, for another minute or so until the sauce has thickened slightly and is just starting to boil. Add the shrimp to the wok and toss through two to three times to mix everything together. Serve immediately.

❗ **TIP:** Use up the salted egg whites leftover here in the Salted Egg Fish Cakes (see page 65) or try adding them to some Garlic and Egg-Fried Rice (see page 34), in place of the light soy sauce for something a bit punchier and more fragrant.

Just after we opened School of Wok a slightly loud, bespectacled man approached me asking whether I would be interested in helping to create a menu for his new line of Chinese takeouts. After numerous discussions with him about his fresh ideas on takeout food, it soon became our mission to show people they deserve better than the mediocre, greasy fare from the local takeout that we have all become much too comfortable with and accepting of. So I created this dish, along with many others for his now successful restaurant. Note to self: always trust a man with thick-rimmed glasses … or at least his recipe for success.

ZING ZING TEMPURA SEA BASS

SERVES: 2
PREPARATION TIME: 30 MINUTES
COOKING TIME: 10 MINUTES

5 dried red chiles
2 garlic cloves
1 scallion
1 tsp Sichuan peppercorns
2 x 3½ to 5¼ oz (100 to 150 g) sea bass
   fillets, skin on
Vegetable oil, for frying

The Batter
Scant 1 cup (100 g) all-purpose flour
2 Tbsp (20 g) cornstarch
1 egg white
Approximately 1 cup (250 ml) very cold
   club soda

The Sauce
2 Tbsp (30 g) granulated sugar, dissolved
   in 3¼ Tbsp (50 ml) hot water
1 Tbsp oyster sauce
1 Tbsp light soy sauce
1 tsp dark soy sauce

PREPARATION

- Put the dried red chiles in a small bowl, cover with hot water, and let soak for 30 minutes, then drain and coarsely chop.

- Finely slice the garlic and cut the scallion into thin rings. Crush the Sichuan peppercorns with a mortar and pestle or whiz them together in a spice grinder or coffee grinder to form a powder.

- Keeping the skin on, slice the fish fillets into large diagonal pieces roughly 1¼ in (3 cm) wide.

- Mix the sauce ingredients together in a bowl or ramekin.

- To make the batter, sift the flours together in a separate bowl, add the egg white, and mix well.

✤ BUILD YOUR WOK CLOCK: place your fish pieces at 12 o'clock, then arrange the garlic, Sichuan peppercorns, chiles, sauce bowl, and scallion clockwise around your plate.

COOKING

- Half-fill a large pot, wok, or deep-fryer with vegetable oil and heat to 350°F (180°C), or until the tip of a wooden chopstick or skewer starts to fizz after a second or so in the oil.

- Pour the cold club soda into the batter and mix well with a whisk until smooth and thin with the consistency of light cream.

- Dip the fish chunks into the batter, then carefully lower them into the preheated oil and fry for 3 minutes, or until golden brown. Remove the fish pieces carefully with a slotted spoon and drain well on a plate covered with paper towels.

- In a separate wok, heat 1 Tbsp of vegetable oil until smoking. Add the garlic and stir-fry for 20 seconds until it starts to brown. Add the Sichuan peppercorns and dried red chiles, then pour over the sauce and bring to a vigorous boil. Add the fish pieces and toss through two to three times to mix everything together. Transfer to a serving plate and sprinkle over the scallion to finish. Serve immediately.

! **TIP:** Do not keep the fish in the wok any longer than it takes to toss through two or three times, or it will start to lose its crispiness due to excess heat and moisture.

Cooking something like this at home is indeed adventurous! This is a great dish for a small dinner party—serve it with some slow-cooked meat, simple greens, and rice on the side and you'll have a wonderfully balanced meal. If cooked well, the skin and even bones of the fins become so crispy that you should be able to just crunch through them with your teeth. Unless it is incredibly small, deep-frying a whole fish can only be done well in a good-size wok.

CRISPY BREAM WITH PICKLED RED ONION AND SWEET CHILI DRESSING

SERVES: 4
PREPARATION TIME: 20 MINUTES PLUS PICKLING
COOKING TIME: 15 MINUTES

1 x 1 lb 2 oz (500 g) sea bream, scaled, cleaned, and degilled (ask the fish supplier to do this for you)
A thumb-size piece of ginger
1⅔ cups (200 g) cornstarch, seasoned with ¼ tsp salt and ¼ tsp black pepper
Vegetable oil, for frying

Red Onion Pickle
½ small red onion, finely sliced
4 Tbsp rice vinegar
1 tsp granulated sugar
½ tsp salt

The Sauce
3 Tbsp sweet chili sauce
1 Tbsp light soy sauce
2 Tbsp rice vinegar
1 Tbsp granulated sugar
A dash of dark soy sauce
3 Tbsp water

PREPARATION

- To make the pickle, put all the pickle ingredients in a bowl and mix together well. Set aside for at least 30 minutes.

- Make 3 diagonal cuts with a sharp knife in either side of the fish through the skin. (These cuts should be deep enough to hit the bones and will open up the flesh slightly.) Place the fish in a large bowl.

- Cut the ginger into fine matchsticks and sprinkle them inside the fish cavity and all over the fish itself. Add the seasoned cornstarch and rub it into all the cracks, over the head, inside the cavity, and into the slashes that you have cut, until the whole fish is evenly covered.

- Mix all the sauce ingredients together in a separate bowl or ramekin.

COOKING

- Half-fill a large pot, wok, or deep-fryer with vegetable oil and heat to 350°F (180°C), or until the tip of a wooden chopstick or skewer starts to fizz after a second or so in the oil.

- Carefully lay the seasoned fish into the hot oil, ensuring it is covered entirely, and deep-fry for 1 to 2 minutes. Reduce the heat slightly to around 325°F (160°C) and continue to deep-fry for another 8 to 10 minutes until the fish is cooked through and is golden brown all the way to its tail. Remove the fish carefully with a pair of tongs and drain well on a plate covered with paper towels.

- Meanwhile, put the sauce in a separate saucepan or small wok and bring to a vigorous boil over high heat. Once boiling, remove from the heat and pour over the cooked fish. Spoon over the pickled red onion slices and serve.

! TIP: Cutting the slits into the sides of the fish greatly speeds up the cooking process, while starting the deep-frying process at a higher heat and then reducing the temperature of the oil ensures that the fish will cook through without the risk of burning the outside.

The Chinese have been in Malaysia for over ten generations now and continue to cook up and deep-fry the abundance of seafood around the country. This dish takes its influence from a type of large shrimp called mantis shrimp that is very popular in Kota Kinabalu, East Malaysia, where we used to travel to as a family. Langoustines, with their sweet flesh, make a good substitute. The only hard work here is in the cleaning and picking at the meat once cooked, but if you are happy to do so, it's well worth the adventure!

CRISPY LANGOUSTINES WITH COCONUT SHALLOT CRUNCH

SERVES: 2 TO 4 WITH SIDES
PREPARATION TIME: 45 MINUTES
COOKING TIME: 10 MINUTES

1 lb 2 oz (500 g) langoustines
Scant 1 cup (100 g) cornstarch, seasoned
  with ¼ tsp salt and ¼ tsp pepper
3 garlic cloves
1 fresh Thai chile
A handful of cilantro
¼ tsp salt
½ tsp freshly ground black pepper
Vegetable oil, for frying

Coconut Shallot Crunch
½ cup (50 g) dry unsweetened coconut
1¾ oz (50 g) ready-fried shallots
2 Tbsp Chinese five-spice
1 tsp salt
4 tsp granulated sugar

PREPARATION

- Wash the langoustines thoroughly and dry with a clean dish towel. Using a pair of cooking scissors, insert the point in between the head and the body, then cut down the length of the shell from head to tail. Open up the langoustines and clean out the intestinal tract with a toothpick as if you were deveining an ordinary shrimp (see page 40).

- Place the langoustines in a bowl with the seasoned cornstarch. Cover the bowl with a plate or lid, hold together firmly, and shake to mix the cornstarch well into the langoustines.

- Mince the garlic and chiles. Coarsely chop the cilantro.

- For the coconut shallot crunch, toast the dry unsweetened coconut in a dry frying pan over medium heat for 4 to 5 minutes until evenly golden brown, then add to a spice grinder, coffee grinder, or mortar and pestle with the remaining ingredients and grind the mixture to a fine powder.

✸ BUILD YOUR WOK CLOCK: place your langoustines at 12 o'clock, then arrange the garlic, chile, salt and pepper, coconut shallot crunch bowl, and cilantro clockwise around your plate.

COOKING

- Half-fill a large pot, wok, or deep-fryer with vegetable oil and heat to 338°F (170°C), or until the tip of a wooden chopstick or skewer starts to fizz after 2 to 3 seconds in the oil. Carefully add the langoustines and deep-fry for 5 to 6 minutes until coral pink on the inside and golden brown on the outside. Remove the pieces carefully with a slotted spoon and drain well on a plate covered with paper towels.

- In a separate wok, heat 1 Tbsp of vegetable oil over high heat until smoking-hot. Add the garlic, chile, salt, and pepper, then add the langoustines and 3 Tbsp of the coconut shallot crunch and toss together a few times. Transfer to a serving plate and sprinkle over another 1 to 2 Tbsp of the coconut shallot crunch and the cilantro. Serve immediately.

❗ TIP: The coconut shallot crunch here makes more than you need for the recipe but is great thrown over stir-fries, broiled meat, or other seafood dishes such as the Steamed Scallops with Garlic and Vermicelli (see page 88). Keep it in an airtight container until needed.

Until starting School of Wok I had actually never cooked a crispy chili beef, as it isn't really something that I tend to associate with homecooked Chinese food but rather late-night takeout. I originally created it for some of my most loyal customers who were huge advocates of the dish and then, soon after learning this recipe, the school. I now have a bit of a soft spot for it, as without it, School of Wok may not have had the opportunity to become the success that it is.

SUCCULENT CRISPY CHILI BEEF

SERVES: 4
PREPARATION TIME: 20 MINUTES
COOKING TIME: 10 MINUTES

7 oz (200 g) sirloin
3⅓ cups (400 g) cornstarch seasoned with
　½ tsp salt and ½ tsp black pepper
A thumb-size piece of ginger
3 garlic cloves
2 fresh Thai chiles
A large handful of cilantro
Vegetable oil, for frying

The Marinade
2 tsp sesame oil
1 tsp granulated sugar
2 Tbsp light soy sauce
1 egg

The Sauce
½ Tbsp dark soy sauce
3 Tbsp tomato ketchup
6 Tbsp Chinkiang black
　rice vinegar
4 Tbsp honey

PREPARATION

- Cut the meat into thin strips roughly ⅛ in (3 mm) wide and place in a mixing bowl. Add the marinade ingredients and, using your hands, massage the pieces until they are evenly coated, then add the seasoned cornstarch and rub it into the meat. The meat will stick together in clumps at first but will start to separate as you continue to massage it. Once all the meat has completely separated it is ready to be fried.

- Finely dice the ginger, garlic, and chiles and mince the cilantro. Mix all the sauce ingredients together in a small bowl or ramekin.

- ❇ BUILD YOUR WOK CLOCK: place your meat bowl at 12 o'clock, then arrange the ginger, garlic, chile, sauce bowl, and cilantro clockwise around your plate.

COOKING

- Half-fill a large pot, wok, or deep-fryer with vegetable oil and heat to 350°F (180°C), or until the tip of a wooden chopstick or skewer starts to fizz after a second or so in the oil.

- Carefully add the marinated meat and deep-fry until golden brown, about 2 to 3 minutes. Remove the pieces carefully with a slotted spoon and drain well on a plate covered with paper towels.

- In a separate wok, heat ½ Tbsp of vegetable oil over high heat until smoking-hot. Add the ginger, garlic, and chile, lower the heat to medium, and stir-fry for 30 seconds until fragrant.

- Pour over the sauce mixture and bring to a vigorous boil, then add the crispy meat and give the wok two or three tosses to mix everything together. Spoon into a serving bowl and sprinkle over the cilantro to finish. Serve immediately.

- ❗ TIP: Popping your sirloin in the freezer 30 minutes before slicing will harden the meat and make it much easier to cut into even-size pieces.

No matter how much I forget as I get older, I have a steel-trap memory for food. This ability to recall selective food experiences has been passed down to me from my parents—memories in the Pang family, it seems, always hold hands with our sense of smell and taste. One of these, a plate of crispy garlic chicken wings from the "aunty" at the poolside café by our apartment block in Singapore, has remained in the minds of both my sisters and myself since we were served it some twenty-odd years ago. To this day I cannot figure out how she ever made something so simple taste just so good. Here is my best attempt.

CHILDHOOD CHICKEN WINGS WITH STICKY CHILI DIP

SERVES: 2
PREPARATION TIME: 20 MINUTES PLUS MARINATING
COOKING TIME: 10 MINUTES

8 chicken wings (halved or kept whole
   depending on how you want to serve)
Vegetable oil, for frying

The Marinade
3 garlic cloves, finely sliced
¼ tsp Chinese five-spice
½ tsp granulated sugar
1 tsp salt
½ tsp black pepper

The Batter
1 egg white
½ cup (50 g) cornstarch
A pinch of sea salt
A pinch of ground black pepper
Scant 1 Tbsp (25 ml) cold water
1 Tbsp black sesame seeds

Sticky Chili Dip
1 Tbsp sriracha chili sauce or Korean
   chili paste
1 Tbsp hoisin sauce
1 Tbsp Chinkiang black rice vinegar
1 Tbsp sesame seeds

PREPARATION
- Wash the chicken wings thoroughly, then dry them with a clean dish towel and put them in a bowl. Add the marinade ingredients and, using your hands, massage them into the meat. Cover with plastic wrap and let marinate in the refrigerator for at least 1 hour, or overnight for best results.

- Once the chicken wings have marinated, mix the batter ingredients together in a bowl, then add to the wings and mix together well until evenly coated.

- Mix all the dipping sauce ingredients together in a small bowl or ramekin.

COOKING
- Half-fill a large pot, wok, or deep-fryer with vegetable oil and heat to 325°F (160°C), or until the tip of a wooden chopstick or skewer starts to bubble (but not fizz) after 2 to 3 seconds in the oil.

- Carefully add the wings and deep-fry for 8 to 10 minutes, or until the wings are golden brown and fully cooked. Remove the wings from the oil and drain well on paper towels. Serve immediately, alongside the dipping sauce.

! **TIP:** To check if the chicken wings are fully cooked, remove one from the oil and pierce it through the middle of the thickest part with a skewer or sharp knife—the meat should be white all the way through.

This alternative sweet-and-sour dish always brings back happy memories, as the first time I cooked it was for my very own wedding. Believe it or not, the School of Wok staff, my sisters, and I prepped up enough food for 200 guests the day before the big event. If my wife wasn't tipped off beforehand that she was marrying a slightly crazy man, this certainly did the trick! The first thing we had to do to prepare this dish was dry-roast the pineapple—a process that gives the dish its unique flavor.

CHARRED PINEAPPLE CHICKEN IN SWEETENED BLACK RICE VINEGAR

SERVES: 2 TO 4
PREPARATION TIME: 1 HOUR
COOKING TIME: 15 MINUTES

7 oz (200 g) fresh pineapple or drained
    canned pineapple
10½ oz (300 g) boned, skinless chicken
    thighs
1⅔ cups (200 g) cornstarch, seasoned with
    ¼ tsp salt and ¼ tsp black pepper
1 onion
1 green bell pepper
2 Tbsp sesame seeds
Vegetable oil, for frying

The Marinade
1 tsp sesame oil
½ tsp granulated sugar
¼ tsp Chinese five-spice
1 Tbsp light soy sauce
1 egg

The Sauce
4 Tbsp Chinkiang black rice vinegar
2 Tbsp granulated sugar
1 Tbsp dark soy sauce
⅞ cup (200 ml) chicken broth

PREPARATION

- Preheat the oven to 450°F (230°C).

- Cut the pineapple into large chunks, peeling it and setting aside the peelings if using fresh pineapple as you go. Put the pineapple chunks on a roasting tray and cook in the preheated oven for 20 minutes, or until charred around the edges. Set aside.

- Lay your chicken thighs flat and slice them at an angle into thin pieces roughly 2 in (5 cm) wide. Put the meat in a mixing bowl, add the marinade ingredients, and mix together well, then add the seasoned cornstarch and, using your hands, massage it into the meat until each piece of meat separates.

- Put all the sauce ingredients in a saucepan, adding your discarded pineapple pieces if using fresh pineapple, and bring to a boil. Lower the heat and simmer for 15 minutes, then increase the heat to a boil and cook for a another 5 minutes until the flavors have melded and infused and the sauce has reduced by half. Remove the pineapple pieces and pour into a small bowl.

- Chop the onion and bell pepper into large chunks. Toast the sesame seeds in a dry wok for 2 to 3 minutes until fragrant and golden brown, then set aside.

- 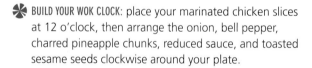 BUILD YOUR WOK CLOCK: place your marinated chicken slices at 12 o'clock, then arrange the onion, bell pepper, charred pineapple chunks, reduced sauce, and toasted sesame seeds clockwise around your plate.

COOKING

- Half-fill a large pot, wok, or deep-fryer with vegetable oil and heat to 338°F (170°C), or until the tip of a wooden chopstick or skewer starts to fizz after a few seconds in the oil. Carefully add the marinated chicken and deep-fry until golden brown, about 4 to 5 minutes. Remove the pieces carefully with a slotted spoon and drain on a plate covered with paper towels.

- In a separate wok, heat 1 Tbsp of vegetable oil over high heat until smoking-hot. Add the onion and pepper and stir-fry for 1 minute until nicely charred. Add the pineapple chunks, pour over the sauce, and bring to a vigorous boil, then add the chicken pieces and toss through two to three times to mix everything together. Spoon into a serving bowl, sprinkle over the toasted sesame seeds, and serve.

In the old days (way before the internet), sweet-and-sour was not red in color at all, as it was predominantly made up of vinegar, sugar, and dark soy sauce. However, with the heavy influence Western culture now has, the Cantonese have found that ketchup provides the perfect balance and wrapping consistency for this dish. Who's to say this recipe upgrade isn't just as authentic as the old ways? As with any culture as it changes and adapts, it doesn't make its expressions any less authentic; it just makes them a product of the times.

CLASSIC SWEET-AND-SOUR PORK

SERVES: 2 TO 4
PREPARATION TIME: 20 MINUTES
COOKING TIME: 10 MINUTES

10½ oz (300 g) pork blade steaks
1⅔ cups (200 g) cornstarch, seasoned with
  ¼ tsp salt and ¼ tsp black pepper
½ onion (optional)
½ green bell pepper (optional)
Vegetable oil, for frying

The Marinade
1 tsp sesame oil
½ tsp granulated sugar
1 Tbsp light soy sauce
1 egg

The Sauce
4 Tbsp tomato ketchup
4 Tbsp rice vinegar or white
  wine vinegar
4 Tbsp granulated sugar
½ tsp dark soy sauce

PREPARATION

- Cut the meat into ¾-in (2-cm) cubes and place in a large mixing bowl. Add the marinade ingredients and, using your hands, massage the pieces until they are evenly coated, then add the seasoned cornstarch and rub it into the meat. The meat will first start to stick together in clumps but will start to separate as you continue to rub it. Once all the meat has completely separated it is ready to be fried.

- Cut the onion and bell pepper, if using, into ¾-in (2-cm) dice. Mix the sauce ingredients together in a small prep bowl or ramekin.

✿ **BUILD YOUR WOK CLOCK:** place your pork dice at 12 o'clock, then arrange the onion and bell pepper, if using, and the sauce bowl clockwise around your plate.

COOKING

- Half-fill a large pot, wokm or deep-fryer with vegetable oil and heat to 350°F (180°C), or until the tip of a wooden chopstick or skewer starts to fizz after a second or so in the oil. Carefully add the marinated meat and deep-fry until golden brown, about 5 to 6 minutes. Remove the pieces carefully with a slotted spoon and drain well on a plate covered with paper towels.

- In a separate wok, heat 1 Tbsp of vegetable oil over high heat until smoking-hot. Add the onion and pepper, if using, and stir-fry for 1 minute until the onions are lightly browned, then pour over the sauce and bring to a vigorous boil.

- Once boiling, add the pork pieces and toss through a few times to mix everything together. Serve immediately.

! **TIP:** The key to a good sweet-and-sour is to ensure the meat is as crispy as possible and that there is just enough sauce to wrap around the meat, but not so much that the meat is swimming in it. If the sauce is not quite sticky or thick enough, continue to boil it in the wok for 30 seconds or so longer before adding the meat.

STEAMING

In Chinese culture and medicine there is a unique adjective used to describe people's internal systems, food, and even environments called YEET HAY. This is a very specific and in-depth concept, with the closest possible literal translation into English being "hot air." It is an almost spiritual belief that our bodies are either hot or cold and that we react to different foods and cooking methods in unique ways due to our chemical balance.

Though different, you might be able to think of it much like the Ayurvedic ideas around your body type or dosha—and how they affect everything you do, from your emotions to your diet. This description does not just apply to people alone. Some cooking techniques such as deep-frying are also considered to be YEET HAY, although this can also change depending on the chemical balance of the person eating it. Steaming, seen from within this cultural context, is considered to be the healthiest form of cooking within Chinese cuisine, because of its delicate balance of heat and moisture.

As with most cooking techniques, steaming is just another way of initially sealing the flavors of what you are cooking first, then cooking them through once the heat begins to penetrate the ingredients. Due to the less intense heat of even the strongest home gas or induction stoves, steam created in a home environment (i.e. from a wok or saucepan placed on a domestic stove) is likely to act as more of an engulfing heat, rather than the high-pressured steam that is created from the serious wok burners or steamers in a Chinese restaurant kitchen.

STEAMING AT HOME: A STEP-BY-STEP GUIDE

When setting up a steam environment at home the best thing to use is a large, flat-bottomed wok with either a steamer stand and lid or a suitable steam basket, which sits directly on top of the wok to collect the steam. There are a number of traditional ways in which you can set up a steamer at home and these can be seen opposite:

❗ TIP: The biggest difference between a bamboo steam basket and a stainless-steel steamer with a glass or metal lid is that the bamboo lid collects any condensation, therefore preventing any water droplets forming on the inside of the lid and dropping back down onto the food. This is very useful when steaming things like dumplings, helping to keep the dough intact.

SETUP 1: WOK, STEAMER STAND AND LID

1. Fill your wok a third of the way up with hot water.

2. Place a steamer stand in the wok.

3. Place your plate of food on top, ensuring there is space between the plate and the edge of the wok so that the steam can engulf the food.

4. Bring the water to a vigorous boil.

5. Place a suitable lid over the top.

SETUP 2: WOK AND STEAM BASKET

1. Fill your wok a third of the way up with hot water.

2. Place either a 10- or 12-in (25- or 30-cm) bamboo steam basket over the top, with your food in a bowl or plate inside the basket, allowing space for the lid to enclose the steam.

3. Cover with the steam basket lid.

Recipe testing for me is always slightly intimidating as it is a true test of your ability to understand chemistry, flavor pairings, and time management. My chef's training doesn't guarantee the dishes will be foolproof—sometimes a bad dish just happens! Such was the case here. I had this wonderful idea of creating a complicated, slightly smoky, steamed sesame eggplant. Sadly, on first test it didn't work and took my wife's lovingly homegrown eggplant with it. Lesson learned: sometimes the success of a dish lies in its simplicity, like in this final version.

STEAMED EGGPLANT WITH SCALLION AND GARLIC DRESSING

SERVES: 2
PREPARATION TIME: 10 MINUTES
COOKING TIME: 15 MINUTES

10½ oz (300 g) Chinese eggplants or
   regular eggplants
1 tsp salt

Scallion and Garlic Dressing
1 Tbsp light soy sauce
1 Tbsp rice vinegar
1 Tbsp granulated sugar
1 tsp Chiu Chow chili oil
1 tsp sesame oil
1 garlic clove, minced
1 Tbsp minced scallion
1 Tbsp minced cilantro

PREPARATION

- Peel the eggplants and slice them into ¾ by 2-in (2 by 5-cm) thick sticks (thumb-size pieces), put them in a bowl with the salt, and cover with cold water.

- Mix the dressing ingredients together in a bowl or small ramekin until the sugar is fully dissolved.

- Drain the eggplant slices and lay them onto a large plate that will fit in your wok.

COOKING

- Set the wok up with a steamer stand and fill with boiling water to a third of the way up the sides. Place the eggplant plate into the wok, cover with a lid, and steam for 10 to 12 minutes, or until the eggplant is tender.

- Remove the plate from the steamer, pour the dressing over the eggplant, and mix together lightly.

! TIP: To test whether the eggplant is cooked through, insert a fork into one of the pieces. If the fork goes straight through without any trouble, then the eggplant is ready to serve.

When it comes to learning about Chinese dumplings, wontons are the best starting point. The dough comes ready-made, either fresh or frozen in most Asian grocery stores, and is very much like an egg pasta—made from egg, a medium- to high-gluten wheat flour (similar to all-purpose flour), hot water, and oil. The method of folding below creates a shape much like a gold ingot (pre20th century Chinese currency) and it is said that if you can fold your wontons in such a shape, you are giving your friends and family plenty of good wealth for years to come!

STEAMED WONTONS IN CHILI BROTH

SERVES: 4
PREPARATION TIME: 1 HOUR
COOKING TIME: 10 MINUTES

1 garlic clove
1 scallion
a large handful of cilantro,
    plus extra to garnish
10 to 15 Chinese chives
3 dried shiitake mushrooms, drained
    and soaked (see page 47)
2 leaves of Napa cabbage
5¼ oz (150 g) raw tiger shrimp
    (optional), peeled and deveined (see
    page 40)
1 Tbsp light soy sauce
½ tsp granulated sugar
2 tsp sesame oil
20 wonton pastries

Chili Broth
⅞ cup (200 ml) chicken broth
½ Tbsp oyster sauce
2 tsp Chiu Chow chilli oil

PREPARATION

- Mince the garlic, scallion, cilantro, Chinese chives, soaked shiitake mushrooms, and Napa leaves and place in a mixing bowl. Finely dice the shrimp (if using) and add to the mixing bowl along with the soy sauce, sugar, and sesame oil. Mix everything together.

- Wrap the wontons as described below.

COOKING

- Place all the wontons in a large, deep bowl. Bring the chicken broth to a simmer in a saucepan, then stir in the oyster sauce and chili oil. Pour the broth ingredients over the wontons.

- Set the wok up with a steamer stand and fill with boiling water to a third of the way up the sides. Put the wonton bowl into the wok, cover with a lid, and steam for 6 to 8 minutes until the wontons have shriveled slightly and are cooked through. Remove from the wok and serve garnished with a little chopped cilantro.

! **TIP:** Dumplings like these can be kept in the freezer once made. They must be cooked from frozen for 2 minutes longer than the recommended cooking time when cooking fresh, rather than allowing them to thaw out and lose their shape.

WRAPPING

1. Place 1 tsp of filling in the center of each dough. Using the tip of your finger, wet all sides of the dough with cold water.

2. Fold the bottom corner over the filling to the top corner and press the dumpling down to seal all sides (to form a triangle).

3. Holding the base of the filling with your thumbs, pull the 2 corners of the triangle toward each other, (in the school, we like to call this the "Dark Knight Rising" as it looks roughly like a Batman shape).

4. Overlap the ends and press together to form a "gold ingot / trough" shape. Set aside and fold the rest of the wontons the same way.

SCALLOP SIU MAI

SERVES: 8 TO 10
PREPARATION TIME: 1 HOUR PLUS SOAKING
COOKING TIME: 10 MINUTES

10 fresh king scallops
3½ oz (100 g) shrimp, peeled and
   deveined (see page 40)
2 dried shiitake mushrooms, soaked
   (see page 47)
10½ oz (300 g) ground pork
Scant ¼ cup (20 g) cornstarch
1 pack of fresh wonton pastries

The Marinade
1 Tbsp sesame oil
½ egg white
½ tsp black pepper
½ tsp salt
1 tsp granulated sugar

Dipping Sauce (optional)
2 Tbsp light soy sauce
2 Tbsp Chinkiang black rice vinegar
A small piece of ginger, cut into fine
   matchsticks

PREPARATION

- Remove the scallop roes, if still attached, and slice the scallops in half lengthwise. Finely chop the shrimp and mushrooms. Mix together the sauce ingredients, if using, in a small bowl or ramekin.

- Mix the pork, shrimp, mushrooms, and cornstarch together with the marinade ingredients, then beat the mix together until it forms a smooth paste (see Tip).

- Cut the wonton dough into circles using a 2½-in (6.5-cm) pastry cutter, then place 1½ tsp of the pork mixture in the center of each dough. Using the base of the teaspoon, spread the filling out over the dough, ensuring it covers it completely edge to edge.

- Create an "egg cup" shape with your left hand and insert the dough so that it rests on top, with the middle drooping into the center of your hand. With your right hand, use the base of your spoon as a "lid" to ensure the meat stays in the parcel, while turning the dough with your left hand using your thumb and index finger of your "egg cup." The aim is to form a uniform dumpling with straight walls of dough all the way around the meat. Once your dumplings have been made, place half a scallop on top of each.

COOKING

- Line a bamboo steamer with greased baking parchment or banana leaf. Add the dumplings to the basket, place over a wok a third-filled with boiling water, and steam for 8 to 10 minutes. Serve with with the dipping sauce, if using, or with sweet soy sauce.

! TIP: The traditional way to beat the filling is to scoop it from the mixing bowl in a cupped hand and throw it back into the bowl. This not only tenderizes the meat, but will push any air out of the mix, creating a smooth finish when biting into the dumplings.

STEAMED SCALLOPS WITH GARLIC AND VERMICELLI

SERVES: 2 TO 3
PREPARATION TIME: 20 MINUTES
COOKING TIME: 5 MINUTES

5 garlic cloves
1 scallion
1 x 3½ oz (100 g) nest of dried mung
  bean vermicelli noodles
6 fresh whole king scallops, roes attached,
  cleaned
6 scallop shells (ask your fish supplier
  for these)

The Sauce
1 fresh Thai chile, finely chopped
A thumb-size piece of ginger, sliced
2 garlic cloves, minced
A handful of cilantro leaves, minced
1 scallion, minced
1 tsp chilli oil
1 Tbsp hoisin sauce
2 Tbsp light soy sauce
1 Tbsp dark soy sauce
2 tsp granulated sugar
1 tsp sesame oil

PREPARATION

- Mince the garlic. Slice the scallion into small rings and place in a small bowl for garnishing later.

- Put the vermicelli noodles in a bowl, cover with boiling water, and let soak for 10 minutes until soft. Drain, then cut with scissors into small pieces.

- Arrange the scallop shells on a large plate. Divide the noodles between the scallop shells, then top each with a scallop. Sprinkle over the garlic.

- Mix the sauce ingredients together in a bowl or small ramekin until the sugar is fully dissolved.

COOKING

- Set the wok up with a steamer stand and fill with boiling water to a third of the way up the sides. Place the scallop plate in the wok, cover with a lid, and steam for 3 to 5 minutes, depending on the size of the scallops (see Tip).

- Remove the scallop plate from the wok. Drizzle the sauce over the scallops and sprinkle over the scallion rings to finish.

! **TIP:** To check whether the scallops are cooked, press a finger gently into the scallop meat; if it gives some resistance, the scallop will be cooked through properly.

Fresh river shrimp have a naturally sweet and savory flavor, which means they rarely require any additional marinating or flavoring—just a little steam and a bit of chili sauce on the side. We find these for the school at an inconspicuous fish supplier who dishes out live lobster, crabs, and fresh shrimp to all the local restaurants from his store tucked away behind the main streets in London's Chinatown. If you can't get your hands on river shrimp, fresh regular shrimp work well here too.

STEAMED RIVER SHRIMP WITH HOMEMADE CHILI SAUCE

SERVES: 4
PREPARATION TIME: 15 MINUTES
COOKING TIME: 20 MINUTES

24 river shrimps or fresh shrimp, with shell
   and heads kept intact

Homemade Chili Sauce
A thumb-size piece of ginger
2 scallions
2 large red chiles
6 Tbsp light soy sauce
6 Tbsp water
1 Tbsp dark soy sauce
2 tsp Shaoxing rice wine (optional)
1 Tbsp granulated sugar

PREPARATION

• Devein the shrimp by inserting a toothpick roughly three-quarters of the way up the back of the shrimp and pulling the dark tract up and out of the shell. Arrange the shrimp on a plate.

• Cut the ginger, scallion, and red chiles into fine matchsticks and combine with the remaining chili sauce ingredients.

COOKING

• Place a bamboo steamer over a wok a third filled with boiling water. Put the shrimp plate inside the steamer, cover with the lid, and steam for 8 to 10 minutes, or until the shrimp are pink in color and cooked through.

• Remove from the steamer and serve with the chili sauce on the side.

! TIP: Depending on the size of the shrimp, the steaming process may be quicker than 8 minutes. Shrimp become quite rubbery when overcooked, so be sure to remove the whole shrimp from the heat as soon as they have turned coral pink in color.

An underrated fish, most people tend to avoid skate when they walk past it in the stores, yet it couldn't be easier to deal with when cooking. From its lack of needle-like bones, to its soft, flaky white meat, there just isn't anything else quite like it.

BLACK BEAN SKATE WING

SERVES: 2
PREPARATION TIME: 10 MINUTES
COOKING TIME: 15 MINUTES

1 x 12¼ oz to 1 lb 2 oz (350 to 500 g)
  skate wing
A thumb-size piece of ginger
1 scallion
2 tsp preserved black beans
1 garlic clove
A pinch of salt
2 Tbsp vegetable oil
1 Tbsp light soy sauce

PREPARATION

- Place the skate wing in a dish large enough to sit in your large wok on a steamer stand, with enough space to cover the wok completely with a lid.

- Finely slice the ginger and place on top of the skate. Slice the scallion lengthwise into thin strips and place in a small bowl.

- Give the black beans a quick rinse under cold water, then tip them into another small bowl. Mince the garlic and add to the black beans with the salt. Lightly crush the ingredients together with the back of a teaspoon, then spoon the mixture over the top of the skate, spreading it across the length of the wing.

COOKING

- Set your large wok or steaming pan up with a steamer stand and fill with boiling water to a third of the way up the sides. Place the fish dish into the wok or pan, cover with a lid, and steam for 7 to 15 minutes until the fish is cooked and the flesh is falling off the wing when tested with a fork. Remove the fish from the pan and sprinkle over the scallion.

- Heat the vegetable oil in a frying pan until smoking-hot, then carefully pour the hot oil over the top of the fish. Spoon over the soy sauce and serve.

! TIP: Try not to move fish around too much while cooking—no matter how you do so—the delicate flesh benefits from being barely touched. This dish is best served directly from the dish that it sits on during the steaming process.

Much like a portrait painter, sometimes I am "commissioned" to create a recipe that matches a dish that a student has once eaten. When this happens there is always the challenge of creating something that lives up to expectations—when successful, however, the reward is well worth it. This recipe started out as one of my commissioned pieces. Over the years, I have adapted it slightly, making it more about the fish itself than fulfilling a specific brief. It's delicious and works perfectly served with simple blanched greens on the side.

SEA BASS WITH CRUSHED SOYBEANS AND CHILI SAUCE

SERVES: 2
PREPARATION TIME: 15 MINUTES
COOKING TIME: 20 MINUTES

1 Tbsp salted soybeans
2 garlic cloves
1 Thai chile
A large handful of cilantro
1 x 12¼ oz to 1 lb 2 oz (350 to 500 g) sea bass, scaled, cleaned, and degilled (ask your fish supplier to do this for you)
1 Tbsp vegetable oil

The Sauce
1 tsp chili bean sauce
1 Tbsp hoisin sauce
1 Tbsp Shaoxing rice wine
7 Tbsp (100 ml) chicken or vegetable broth, or hot water
A dash of dark soy sauce

PREPARATION

- Lightly crush the soybeans in a small bowl with the back of a teaspoon. Mince the garlic and chile. Coarsely chop the cilantro.

- Wash the fish, pat dry, and place on a large plate or platter suitable for steaming.

- Mix the sauce ingredients together in a small bowl.

✻ **BUILD YOUR WOK CLOCK:** place the crushed soybeans at 12 o'clock, then arrange the garlic, chile, sauce bowl, and chopped cilantro clockwise around the plate.

COOKING

- Set a large wok or steaming pan up with a steamer stand and fill with boiling water to a third of the way up the sides. Place the fish plate into the wok or pan, cover with a lid, and steam for 7 to 12 minutes until cooked (see Tip). Remove and set aside, covering the fish with foil so it stays warm and moist.

- Drain and dry the wok, add the vegetable oil, and heat until smoking. Add the soybeans and stir-fry for 30 seconds, then add the garlic, chiles, and sauce. Bring to a vigorous boil, then add half the cilantro and continue to cook for 1 minute until the sauce has thickened and reduced by at least a third.

- Pour the sauce over the steamed fish and garnish with the remaining cilantro to serve.

↺ **SWAPSIES:** Salted soybeans are fermented soybeans preserved in brine and can be found in most Chinese grocery stores. They add a nice texture to this sauce, however if you cannot find them, the dish works just as well without.

❗ **TIP:** To check whether your fish is fully cooked, pull the dorsal fin (the one on the back) lightly. If it falls off without any force, the fish will be cooked through to the bone. Remove from the pan and set aside.

For me, a good weekday meal needs to be healthy, quick, easy to prepare, and good value for money —no one wants to use up the food budget on after-work meals rather than long, lingering weekend treats. With its vibrant colors and strong flavors this ticks all the boxes, and is perfect for getting you out of that postwork pasta rut we all get stuck in from time to time.

STEAMED TROUT WITH CHILI BEAN, GARLIC, AND GINGER OIL

SERVES: 2
PREPARATION TIME: 10 MINUTES
COOKING TIME: 10 MINUTES

2 x 5¼ oz (150 g) trout fillets, descaled

Chili Bean, Garlic, and Ginger Oil
2 garlic cloves, finely diced
A large piece of ginger, finely diced
1 scallion, finely diced
½ Tbsp chili bean sauce
¼ tsp salt
¼ tsp granulated sugar
¾ Tbsp vegetable oil

PREPARATION

- For the chili bean, garlic, and ginger oil, mix together all the ingredients apart from the vegetable oil in a heatproof bowl. Heat the vegetable oil in a wok until smoking, then pour over the rest of the chili ginger oil ingredients to sizzle. Stir together well and set aside.

- Place the fish fillets on a suitable plate for steaming.

COOKING

- Set the wok up with a steamer stand and fill with boiling water a third to halfway up the sides. Place the fish fillet plate into the wok, cover with a lid, and steam for 8 to 10 minutes until the fish is cooked. (To test this, poke a toothpick into the thickest part of each fillet—if the toothpick goes through without any struggle, the fish is ready to serve.)

- Remove the plate from the wok and spoon over the chili bean, garlic, and ginger oil to coat the fish fillets well. Serve.

SWAPSIES: If you fancy trying this recipe with another type of fish, salmon fillets or even a white-fish fillet such as sea bass or bream work equally well.

In Chinese tradition, serving a whole fish at the dinner table signifies abundance in life, and if you ever see a Chinese family tucking into a whole steamed fish at a restaurant it is most probably a special occasion of some sort. From a purely culinary perspective, one wonderful thing about this tradition is that the fish itself retains all its moisture and flavor while keeping its delicate texture. In the Far East, the typical fish for this dish would be grouper, but I find gurnard has a very similar flavor and texture. Sea bass and bream are also great alternatives.

WHOLE STEAMED GURNARD WITH GINGER AND SCALLION

SERVES: 2 TO 3
PREPARATION TIME: 10 MINUTES
COOKING TIME: 20 MINUTES

1 x 10½ oz to 1 lb 2 oz (350 to 500 g) fresh gurnard, scaled, cleaned, and degilled (ask your fish supplier to do this for you)
A thumb-size piece of ginger
2 scallions
2 Tbsp light soy sauce
½ tsp granulated sugar
2 Tbsp vegetable oil

PREPARATION

- Place the fish in a steaming dish large enough to sit in your large wok on a steamer stand, with enough space to cover the wok completely with a lid.

- Finely slice the ginger and arrange on top of the fish and inside its cavity.

- Slice the scallions into fine matchsticks and place them in a small prep bowl. Put the soy sauce in a separate small bowl or ramekin, add the sugar, and stir to dissolve.

COOKING

- Set your large wok or steaming pan up with a steamer stand and fill with boiling water to a third of the way up the sides. Place the fish dish into the wok or pan, cover with a lid, and steam for 7 to 15 minutes until the fish is cooked. Remove the fish from the pan and sprinkle over the scallion.

- Heat the vegetable oil in a frying pan until smoking-hot. Carefully pour the hot oil over the scallionn and fish to sizzle, then spoon over the soy sauce mixture and serve.

- **! TIP:** When it comes to cooking whole fish, I tend to categorize them into the following sizes for cooking times: small fish (< 10½ oz/300 g) 7 to 9 minutes; medium fish (10½ to 1 lb 2 oz/300 g to 500 g) 10 to 12 minutes; and large fish (1 lb 2 oz to 1 lb 10 oz/ 500 g to 750 g) 13 to 15 minutes.

I think tofu gets a bad rap sometimes—it seems to be thought of as being almost too healthy and therefore tasteless and unappealing. For the people who say that they do not like the taste of tofu, I think it's just that they haven't had it cooked properly or in the right dish. Silken tofu works perfectly here as it is already very delicate and light in texture and, when steamed, develops a luxurious "melt-in-the-mouth" feeling on the palate. The fish and shrimp mix for the stuffing flavor the tofu well, while preserving its lightness and fine texture.

STEAMED STUFFED TOFU WITH SOY DRESSING

SERVES: 2
PREPARATION TIME: 30 MINUTES
COOKING TIME: 15 MINUTES

1 x 10½ oz (300 g) firm silken tofu block
1 to 2 Tbsp cornstarch
1 scallion, sliced, to garnish
1 to 2 Tbsp vegetable oil
2 Tbsp light soy sauce

The Stuffing
1 garlic clove
1¾ oz (50 g) cod fillet or other white
  fish fillet
3½ oz (100 g) raw shrimp, peeled and
  deveined
A handful of cilantro
1 scallion
Sea salt and freshly ground black pepper

PREPARATION

- For the stuffing, put the garlic clove in a food processor and blend well, then add the fish fillet and shrimp and blend together to form a smooth paste. Spoon the mixture into a bowl.

- Mince the cilantro and scallion and add to the fish mixture. Season with salt and pepper to taste and mix together well. Set aside.

- Cut the tofu block lengthwise into ¾-in (2-cm) thick slices and lay each slice flat on a plate. Using a teaspoon, draw an oval around the inside of each slice, then scoop out half of the tofu to form a "crater." This is where your fish mix will sit, so be careful not to cut all the way through the tofu. Spoon ¼ Tbsp of cornstarch into each tofu "crater" (this will help the stuffing to stay in place).

- Place any excess tofu into the fish mix and stir well to combine, then spoon and spread roughly 1 to 2 tsp of the mix into each slice of tofu, flattening the mix carefully without breaking the tofu. Using a spatula, transfer the stuffed tofu slices to a large plate.

COOKING

- Set the wok up with a steamer stand and fill with boiling water to a third of the way up the sides. Place the stuffed tofu plate into the wok, cover with a lid, and steam for 10 minutes until the shrimp are a pale coral color and the fish mix bounces back when pressed. Remove the plate from the steamer and sprinkle over the sliced scallion.

- Heat the vegetable oil in a small pan until smoking-hot, then pour over the scallion to create a sizzle. Spoon over the soy sauce and serve.

SWAPSIES: To make this dish vegetarian, just swap out the fish and shrimp mix for a combination of minced mushrooms of your choice.

Steam in cooking does not always have to come from water boiling in a pan. In this Hong Kong dish the steam is created from the rice, and there is an art to getting the chicken into it at the right time in order to have it cook through perfectly and give you the textures you'll want—a crispy layer of rice on the bottom of the pot, followed by fluffy, steamed rice in the middle and succulent meat on top.

CLAY-POT CHICKEN AND MUSHROOM RICE WITH CHILI AND GARLIC SAUCE

SERVES: 4
PREPARATION TIME: 20 MINUTES PLUS SOAKING
COOKING TIME: 30 MINUTES

14 oz (400 g) boned, skinless chicken
  thighs
8 dried shiitake mushrooms, soaked and
  drained (see page 47)
1⅓ cups (280 g) jasmine rice
Scant 1½ cups (340 ml) water
A thumb-size piece of ginger
1 scallion
1½ Tbsp vegetable oil

The Marinade
2 tsp sesame oil
2 Tbsp light soy sauce
2 Tbsp Shaoxing rice wine
1 tsp granulated sugar
1 Tbsp cornstarch

Chili and Garlic Sauce
½ Tbsp vegetable oil
1 large fresh red chile, coarsely chopped
2 garlic cloves, bashed and peeled
  but kept whole
6 Tbsp dark soy sauce
1 Tbsp granulated sugar

PREPARATION

- To make the chili and garlic sauce, heat the vegetable oil in a small saucepan over medium heat. Add the chile and garlic and cook, stirring, for 30 seconds, then add the soy sauce and sugar to the pan, bring to a boil, and cook for another 30 seconds, until the sauce has caramelized slightly but is still runny. Pour into a ramekin ready for later.

- Cut the chicken thighs into ¼-in (5-mm) slices and put in a bowl. Cut the drained, soaked mushrooms into fine slices and add to the chicken slices. Add the marinade ingredients to the bowl and, using your hands, rub them together until all the marinade has been absorbed.

- Rinse the rice 2 to 3 times to get rid of any excess starch, then drain the rice through a strainer. Measure out the water for cooking in a pitcher. Finely slice the ginger and scallion.

❋ BUILD YOUR WOK CLOCK: place your ginger at 12 o'clock, then arrange the rice, water, marinated chicken bowl, and scallion clockwise around your plate.

COOKING

- Heat the vegetable oil to a medium heat in a clay pot or heavy saucepan. Add the slices of ginger to the oil and stir-fry for 30 seconds until fragrant.

- Add the washed rice to the pan and fry it in the oil for 1 minute, stirring to coat the grains evenly, then pour over the water. Bring to a boil, then reduce to a simmer, add the chicken and mushroom mix, and cook, covered, over low heat for 20 minutes.

- Remove the lid and check that the chicken is cooked (it should be light brown or white in color, with no pink), and that the rice has formed a crisp, golden brown layer on the bottom of the pan. If it needs it, let it cook for a few minutes longer.

- Once cooked, spoon into bowls and garnish with the scallion. Serve with the chili and garlic sauce.

❗ **TIP:** If you hear light "crackling" noises from the bottom of the pan during the last stage of cooking, this is a good sign that the rice is crisping up on the bottom of the pan. If, however, you smell burning, turn the stove off at this point and serve immediately!

Lotus leaves have a porous nature that makes them perfect for steaming—as the steam soaks through them their sweet, earthy aroma is added to whatever is wrapped inside. Here they accentuate the naturally warm flavors of the five-spice and wind-dried sausage, while the lotus root adds a nice contrast in texture. This is a great dinner-party dish; serve the lotus parcels whole and let the guests unwrap their individual parcels.

FIVE-SPICE LOTUS LEAF CHICKEN WITH CHINESE SAUSAGE

SERVES: 6
PREPARATION TIME: 30 MINUTES PLUS SOAKING
COOKING TIME: 30 MINUTES

6 large lotus leaves, soaked in hot water
2 x 3¼ to 4-in (8 to 10-cm) lotus root segment
10 boneless chicken thighs
2 wind-dried Chinese sausages
20 dried golden lily mushrooms, soaked and drained (see page 47)

The Marinade
½ tsp Chinese five-spice
2 Tbsp Shaoxing rice wine
3 Tbsp light soy sauce
2 tsp granulated sugar
2 tsp sesame oil
2 Tbsp cornstarch

PREPARATION

- Put the lotus leaves in a large bowl, cover with hot water, and let soak for at least 30 minutes or up to 1 hour. Peel the lotus root segments and finely slice them into large rings.

- Cut the chicken thighs into eighths and place the pieces in a mixing bowl, then finely slice the wind-dried Chinese sausages and add to the chicken along with the drained soaked mushrooms. Add the marinade ingredients to the bowl and, using your hands, massage them into the meat until everything is well combined.

- To assemble the lotus leaf wraps, lay a leaf on a clean counter and arrange a few of the lotus root slices in the center. Spoon some of the marinated meat over the lotus root, then wrap the edges of the leaves around the meat to form a tight package. Repeat with the remaining leaves.

COOKING

- Place a bamboo steamer over a wok a third filled with boiling water. Put the lotus leaf wraps inside the steamer, cover with a lid, and steam for 25 minutes.

- Remove the wraps from the steamer and serve with rice and a pickled vegetable dish such as Pickled Carrot and Daikon (see page 148).

! **TIP:** You will find lotus root in most Chinese grocery stores; they usually come vacuum-packed. You want to look for lotus root that is light brown in color—try to avoid the black-skinned lotus roots as they tend to be older and not as fresh.

↻ **SWAPSIES:** If you cannot find dried golden lily mushrooms, swap out finely sliced dried porcini, shiitake, or straw mushrooms instead.

Chef Kampo has become my go-to mentor for food advice. Even after spending over 35 years in professional kitchens, his home palate is just as humble, warming, and generous as the man himself. Although an acquired texture to those who are not used to eating it, the yam in this dish adds a certain substantial "stickiness" to the sauce that will satisfy and comfort on a cold winter night. This is true home-style Chinese cooking at its best.

KAMPO'S PORK BELLY AND YAM WITH HOISIN SCALLION SAUCE

SERVES: 4
PREPARATION TIME: 30 MINUTES
COOKING TIME: 1 HOUR 15 MINUTES

1 x 14 oz (400 g) pork belly piece
3 scallions
A thumb-size piece of ginger
1 large yam or sweet potato
1 to 2 Tbsp vegetable oil

The Sauce
2 Tbsp hoisin sauce
2 tsp dark soy sauce
2 Tbsp light soy sauce
4 Tbsp Shaoxing rice wine

PREPARATION

- Bring a large pan of water to a boil, add the whole pork belly, and blanch for 10 minutes. Drain and cool in a bowl of cold water before draining again and slicing into ½-in (1-cm) thick slices.

- Finely slice the scallions and ginger. Peel and slice the yam or sweet potato into ¼-in (5-mm) thick slices. Mix the sauce ingredients together in a bowl.

- Arrange the pork belly and yam slices one by one alternately across a plate—much like stacking CDs along a shelf—until you have used up all the pork.

COOKING

- Heat the oil in a wok over medium heat. Add two-thirds of the scallion and ginger to the wok and stir-fry for 1 minute until everything is aromatic and the scallion is starting to brown. Pour the sauce ingredients into the wok and bring to a boil, then reduce to a simmer and cook for 1 to 2 minutes until the sauce has reduced by about a third. Pour the sauce over the layered pork and yam.

- Set the wok up with a steamer stand and fill with boiling water to halfway up the sides. Place the layered pork and yam plate into the wok, cover with a lid, and steam for about 1 hour until the yam and pork pieces are fragrant and tender. Sprinkle over the remaining scallion to garnish.

! **TIP:** Because this recipe involves such a long period of steaming, check the water every 10 minutes to make sure the wok hasn't run dry, adding a little extra hot water if necessary.

The most common way to eat these ribs is as a type of dim sum, but they also make a great simple meaty meal served with some stir-fried bok choy and rice on the side. Traditionally, sodium bicarbonate and water are used to tenderize the meat; however I have found that leaving the ribs in the marinade overnight and steaming them for a longer period of time works just as well, with the benefit of keeping the natural texture of the meat.

BLACK BEAN SPARE RIBS

SERVES: 4
PREPARATION TIME: 10 MINUTES PLUS MARINATING
COOKING TIME: 30 MINUTES

15 pork ribs, chopped into 1¼- to 1½-in
   (3- to 4-cm) chunks (ask your butcher to
   do this for you)
1 large fresh red chile, finely sliced
1 scallion, finely sliced

The Marinade
2 garlic cloves, minced
2 Tbsp preserved black beans, crushed
2 Tbsp plum sauce
2 Tbsp water
1 tsp salt
2 tsp granulated sugar
1 tsp Chiu Chow chili oil
2 tsp sesame oil
1 tsp black pepper
1 Tbsp cornstarch

PREPARATION

- Put the ribs in a large bowl, add all the marinade ingredients and, using your hands, mix everything together until the ribs are well coated. Cover with plastic wrap and let marinate in the refrigerator for at least 1 hour, preferably overnight.

COOKING

- When you're ready to cook, place a bamboo steamer over a wok a third filled with boiling water. Put the ribs inside the steamer and sprinkle over half of the red chile. Cover with the lid and steam for a minimum of 20 minutes, or until the ribs are tender and light brown in color.

- Remove the ribs from the steamer, sprinkle over the scallion and remaining red chile, and serve.

! **TIP:** To check the ribs are properly cooked, check the ends of the bones—if these are dark in color with no red present then the ribs will be ready.

POACHING AND BRAISING

The vast majority of Chinese cooking methods, like those that we have already touched on, tend to be incredibly quick ways of cooking. While these may be the most commonly used methods of cooking in restaurants and takeouts, prized for their quick turnover nature, Chinese home cooking also allows for slower processes like poaching and braising. These techniques are great for getting different textures and flavors into your dish —with both relying on hot, bubbling liquids surrounding the ingredients inside the cooking vessel as their main source of heat for cooking.

Poaching is used commonly when trying to preserve an ingredient's natural flavor and texture, while braising is a slower cooking method, often used to infuse additional and intense flavors into the ingredient, as well as its surrounding cooking liquid, over a long period of time.

POACHING: A STEP-BY-STEP GUIDE

Poaching or "soft boiling" is a very time-sensitive cooking method—think about the difference between hard-boiling or soft-boiling an egg, for instance. If you know what texture you are aiming to produce from your main ingredient, it will directly reflect how long you poach it for. The most common way to poach something, whether in a wok or a saucepan, is to:

1. Fill a pan with water, either with added ingredients to flavor the water (such as ginger, scallion, garlic, or star anise) or without, depending on your recipe.

2. Add your ingredient to the water and apply heat to the pan to seal in the flavor. (**Note:** some ingredients seal better by placing them directly into boiling water whereas other ingredients turn out better poaching from cold water).

3. Continue to poach your ingredient until it is cooked through, following the specific recipes to begin with in order to understand cooking times.

BRAISING:
A STEP-BY-STEP GUIDE

Braising is essentially a simple form of double-cooking, where the main ingredients are often sealed in a light coating of oil before liquid is added to the pan. This initial searing process will help the ingredients retain their natural moisture and flavor. Over time, while braising, these flavors will begin to infuse into the liquid they are being cooked in, and vice-versa, resulting in a flavorsome dish. Generally, braising methods follow these simple principles:

1. Heat 1 to 2 Tbsp of oil in a heavy saucepan or clay pot to medium heat.

2. Add your spices or marinated meats.

3. Add a sauce, braising liquid, or broth to the pan.

4. Bring to a boil and simmer for as long as the ingredients will stay together.

Cooking eggplant can be a bit of task; due to its spongelike nature it can turn out very oily or even rubbery if undercooked or sealed the wrong way. Here the initial frying off of the eggplant works in the same way as searing a piece of meat before a slow cook. Sealing each piece and then braising the eggplant enables it to absorb the flavors of the rich sauce more gradually, while cooking through evenly.

SICHUAN-STYLE EGGPLANT

SERVES: 2
PREPARATION TIME: 30 MINUTES
COOKING TIME: 20 MINUTES

2 Chinese eggplants
2 to 3 Tbsp vegetable oil
2 garlic cloves
1 fresh Thai chile
A small handful of cilantro

The Sauce
1 Tbsp hoisin or yellow bean sauce
½ tsp chili bean paste
1 Tbsp light soy sauce
1 Tbsp rice vinegar
2 tsp granulated sugar
7 Tbsp (100 ml) water
A dash of dark soy sauce

PREPARATION

- Leaving the skin on, cut the eggplant in half lengthwise, then slice into ¾-in (2-cm) thick long batons or 2-in (5-cm) chunks. Place them in a mixing bowl and immediately pour over 1 to 2 Tbsp of vegetable oil. Mix together well.

- Heat a frying pan over medium heat. Add the eggplant pieces and fry, turning, until golden brown and charred (but not burned) on both sides. Remove from the heat and set aside.

- Mince the garlic, chile, and cilantro. Mix all the sauce ingredients together in a bowl.

- **BUILD YOUR WOK CLOCK:** place the garlic at 12 o'clock, then arrange the eggplant pieces, chile, sauce bowl, and cilantro clockwise around the plate.

COOKING

- Heat 1 Tbsp of vegetable oil in a wok over medium heat. Add the garlic and eggplant to the wok, then add the chile and immediately pour over the sauce mixture. Bring to a vigorous boil, then reduce the heat to a gentle simmer and cook for 12 to 15 minutes over low heat, stirring occasionally, until the sauce has caramelized and thickened slightly.

- Spoon onto a serving plate, and sprinkle over the cilantro to finish. Serve.

- **SWAPSIE:** If you cannot find the bright-purple Chinese eggplants, try using eight to ten of the small Indian eggplants instead. As they are much smaller in size, just slice them in half lengthwise and they are ready to use.

There are many different types of tofu available and, though generally similar in flavor, each offers a slightly different texture. By knowing which type best matches which style of cooking, you will be able to keep its unique texture while allowing it to absorb as much flavor as possible. Japanese egg tofu, for example, forms a fantastic golden-brown coating when fried due to its egg content, while rolled beancurd skin or deep-fried tofu squares (known as tofu pok*) are so absorbent they will suck up the flavor of any sauce you cook them in within five or ten minutes.*

BRAISED MIXED MUSHROOM AND TOFU STEW

SERVES: 4
PREPARATION TIME: 20 MINUTES PLUS SOAKING
COOKING TIME: 45 MINUTES

A thumb-size piece of ginger
1 scallion
10½ oz (300 g) fresh straw or oyster
   mushrooms
10 deep-fried tofu squares (or 1 small
   pack of rolled beancurd skin)
10½ oz (300 g) Japanese egg tofu
2 Tbsp vegetable oil
1 star anise
12 dried shiitake mushrooms, soaked and
   drained (see page 47), retaining
   1¼ cups (300 ml) of the mushroom
   soaking water
2 Tbsp vegetarian oyster sauce
1 Tbsp Shaoxing rice wine
A dash of dark soy sauce

PREPARATION

- Slice the ginger and finely slice the scallion into rings. Coarsely tear apart the straw or oyster mushrooms.

- Cut the deep-fried tofu squares in half or, if using beancurd skin, cut into 1¼-in (3-cm) chunks.

- Slice the Japanese egg tofu into ¾-in (2-cm) cylinders. Warm 1 Tbsp of the vegetable oil in a pan over medium-high heat, add the egg tofu pieces, and fry for 2 minutes on each side or until golden brown. Remove from the pan and drain on clean paper towels.

✿ BUILD YOUR WOK CLOCK: place your ginger at 12 o'clock, then arrange the star anise, shiitake mushrooms, oyster sauce, rice wine, mushroom soaking water, dark soy sauce, tofu pieces, fresh oyster or straw mushrooms, and scallion clockwise around your plate.

COOKING

- Heat the remaining 1 Tbsp of vegetable oil in a saucepan or clay pot over medium heat, add the ginger and star anise, and fry for 30 seconds until slightly fragrant.

- Add the shiitake mushrooms and cook for 2 to 3 minutes, then add the oyster sauce and cook, stirring, for another 2 to 3 minutes until the sauce has thickened and caramelized. Pour over the rice wine, soy sauce, and mushroom soaking water and bring to a boil, then reduce the heat to a simmer.

- Add the tofu pieces and let simmer for 10 minutes, stirring occasionally. Add the fresh mushrooms and simmer for another 5 to 10 minutes until the stew has thickened and reduced, the mushrooms have softened, and the tofu has soaked up all the stew's flavors. Remove from the heat, garnish with the scallion, and serve with steamed rice.

! TIP: If the stew is still quite thin and watery after the allotted cooking time, mix together 2 tsp of cornstarch with 1 Tbsp of cold water to make a paste and stir it into your sauce while on the rolling boil. Let it thicken to the desired consistency, then remove from the heat.

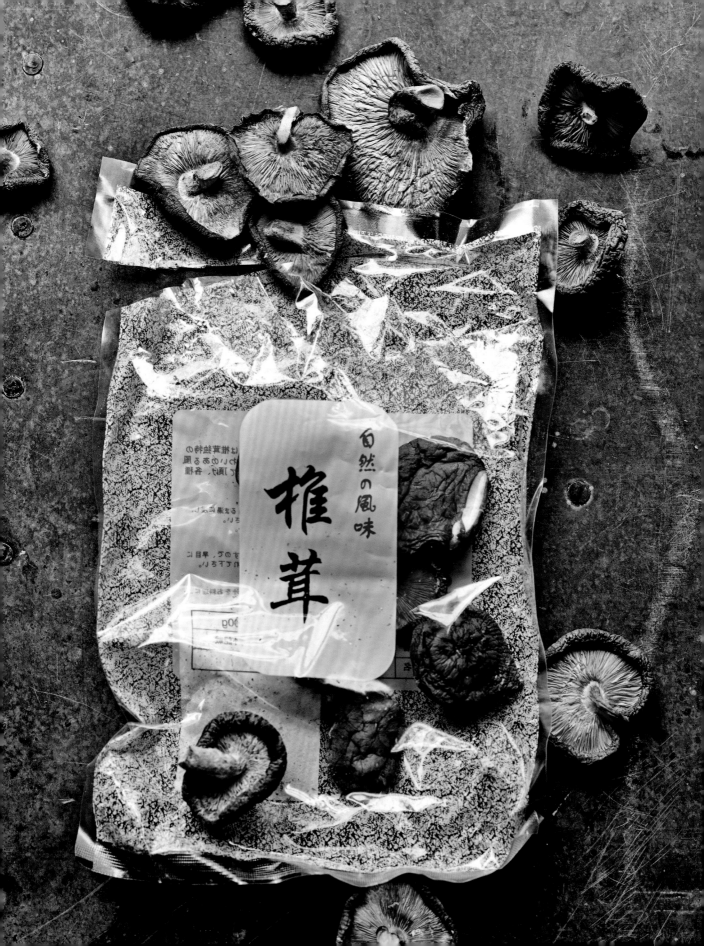

We're so used to seeing squid fried or broiled that many might find the idea of this dish a bit strange. Trust me, take the leap of faith and make it— I promise you won't regret it. Although curries are by no means a Chinese delicacy, this slow-braised squid can be found bubbling away all day in the streets of Hong Kong, where there has been a significant Indian community for many years. The Cantonese have added their own twist to it by sweetening it up with evaporated milk and sugar. Again this might sound strange, but this kind of sweet/savory balance tastes delicious!

BRAISED CURRIED SQUID

SERVES: 2 TO 3
PREPARATION TIME: 20 MINUTES
COOKING TIME: 60 MINUTES

6 Thai shallots
4 garlic cloves
20 whole baby squid, cleaned and quills removed (get your fish supplier to do this for you)
1 Tbsp Madras curry powder
½ tsp ground turmeric
1 Tbsp sesame oil
1¼ cups (300 ml) chicken broth
7 Tbsp (100 ml) evaporated milk
1 tsp salt
½ Tbsp granulated sugar
1 tsp cumin seeds
1 small cinnamon stick
10 fresh curry leaves (optional)
2 Tbsp vegetable oil

PREPARATION

• Peel and finely dice the Thai shallots and garlic.

• Wash the baby squid thoroughly and place in a bowl.

• Mix the curry powder, turmeric, and sesame oil together in small bowl or ramekin to form a paste. In a separate bowl, mix together the broth, evaporated milk, salt, and sugar.

✱ BUILD YOUR WOK CLOCK: place your Thai shallots at 12 o'clock, then arrange the garlic, cumin seeds, cinnamon stick, curry leaves, if using, curry paste bowl, squid, and lastly your broth and evaporated milk mixture clockwise around your plate.

COOKING

• Heat the vegetable oil in a saucepan over medium heat. Add the Thai shallots and cook, stirring occasionally, for 6 to 8 minutes until softened.

• Add the garlic, cumin seeds, and cinnamon stick to the pan and cook, stirring, for 2 to 3 minutes, or until the cumin seeds start to brown. Add the curry leaves, if using, and curry paste and cook for another minute.

• Add the squid to the pan and fry off in the spices for 1 to 2 minutes before pouring over the broth and evaporated milk mixture. Bring to a boil, then reduce to a gentle simmer and cook, covered, for at least 45 minutes (or up to 1½ hours) over low heat. The sauce will have thickened slightly but should still have a brothy consistency. Serve alongside something hot and crispy like the Shiitake and Chive Dumplings (see page 60) or some crusty French bread for dipping into the sauce.

❗ TIP: If you would like to give this dish more of a street food-style presentation, skewer the squid onto three or four bamboo skewers before cooking and follow the method as before.

This is one of the simplest chicken dishes that you can come across in the Chinese home kitchen—it's great for teaching to kids or young adults getting ready for college or leaving home for the first time. The key to it is to ensure you caramelize the soy sauce and sugar mix well enough before you add the water to the chicken. With that in mind the rest is simple; simply sear, stir, and boil.

SOY SAUCE CHICKEN

SERVES: 2
PREPARATION TIME: 10 MINUTES
COOKING TIME: 35 MINUTES

1 onion
A thumb-size piece of ginger
10½ oz (300 g) chicken thighs
  and/or legs
A pinch of Chinese five-spice
1 Tbsp vegetable oil
1 small handful of cilantro leaves

The Sauce
6 Tbsp dark soy sauce
3 Tbsp granulated sugar
Approximately 1¼ to 2 cups
  (300 to 500 ml) hot water

PREPARATION

- Cut the onion into fine slices and the ginger into fine matchsticks. Coarsely chop the cilantro leaves.

- Mix the dark soy sauce with the sugar in a bowl.

- ✺ **BUILD YOUR WOK CLOCK:** place the chopped onions at 12 o'clock, then arrange the ginger, chicken, five-spice, soy sauce mixture, and cilantro clockwise around the plate.

COOKING

- Heat the vegetable oil in a saucepan over medium heat. Add the onion and ginger and cook, stirring for 2 to 3 minutes, or until the onion starts to brown.

- Add the chicken pieces and fry for 4 to 5 minutes, turning over as necessary, until golden brown on all sides, then add the five-spice, soy and sugar mixture, and bring to the boil, stirring well to dissolve the sugar. Reduce the heat to a simmer and cook for another 4 to 5 minutes until the sauce has thickened and caramelized, stirring to ensure the chicken pieces are evenly coated.

- Add just enough hot, but not boiling water to cover the chicken pieces. Bring to a boil, then reduce the heat and let simmer, covered, for 15 minutes. Remove the lid and continue to simmer for 10 minutes, stirring occasionally, until the sauce has reduced by half and is dark, sticky, and caramelized. Transfer to a serving bowl or plate and garnish with the cilantro. Serve.

- ❗ **TIP:** Try adding a few greens here by throwing a bag of green beans or sugar snap peas into the pot 3 minutes before serving.

Beef brisket noodle soup is a classic midnight feast in southern China. The best time to eat this is late at night, as the beef has been cooking away in its fragrant, thick broth since the morning and will be so succulent you won't be able to resist it. The longer you braise this, the better it will taste.

BRAISED BEEF BRISKET SOUP

SERVES: 2 TO 3
PREPARATION TIME: 20 MINUTES PLUS MARINATING
COOKING TIME: 2 TO 3 HOURS

10½ oz (300 g) beef brisket or shin
3½ oz (100 g) hor fun noodles
A thumb-size piece of ginger
A large handful of cilantro
½ daikon
1¼ cups (300 ml) chicken or beef broth
1 Tbsp vegetable oil

The Marinade
1 Tbsp light soy sauce
1 Tbsp oyster sauce
1 Tbsp yellow bean paste or
   yellow bean sauce
1 Tbsp Shaoxing rice wine
½ tsp Chinese five-spice
½ tsp granulated sugar
1 tsp sesame oil
½ Tbsp cornstarch

PREPARATION

- Cut the beef into ¾-in (2-cm) cubes and put in a bowl. Add the marinade ingredients and, using your hands, massage them into the beef pieces until they are well coated. Cover with plastic wrap, place in the refrigerator, and let marinate for a minimum of 1 hour, or preferably overnight.

- Put the noodles in a bowl, cover with boiling water, and let soak for 12 minutes. Drain and set aside.

- Finely slice the ginger and mince the cilantro. Peel the daikon and cut it into 1¼-in (3-cm) chunks.

- ❋ **BUILD YOUR WOK CLOCK:** place the sliced ginger at 12 o'clock, then arrange the beef bowl, broth, daikon, noodles, and cilantro clockwise around the plate.

COOKING

- Heat the vegetable oil in a saucepan over medium-high heat. Add the ginger and marinated beef to the pan and cook for 5 minutes, stirring continuously, until the beef starts to brown on all sides.

- Pour over the broth and bring to a boil, then reduce the heat to a simmer and cook, covered, for 2 to 3 hours over low heat until the the meat is tender and beginning to fall apart. Add the daikon chunks, bring the broth back to a rolling boil, then reduce the heat to a simmer and cook for another 30 minutes.

- Divide the noodles between bowls and ladle over the stew. Sprinkle over the cilantro to garnish. Serve.

- ⟲ **SWAPSIES:** A mild-flavored winter radish, daikon can be found in Chinese grocers and grocery stores. If you cannot find daikon, swap it out with fresh turnip of any shape or size.

- ❗ **TIP:** The longer the beef boils, the more succulent it will be. If you want to add some greens to the dish, place some fresh lettuce and bean sprouts into the serving bowls along with the noodles just before you pour the soup over the top. This will cook the vegetables through without losing their crunch.

There are some things we miss dearly from the days when Grandma Pang was alive, most of them (as tends to be the case with our family) food-related. These See Ji Tau, or "lionhead" meatballs, with their unique texture and comforting flavors, are one of her standout dishes. Grandma only ever made them in massive quantities—it was as though, when cooking them, she couldn't quite figure out when to stop, worried someone might be a bit hungrier than she had planned. Whatever the reason, this warming, winter one-pot-wonder is something I recommend cooking enough for everyone to have at least seconds, if not thirds.

GRANDMA'S "LIONHEAD" MEATBALLS

SERVES: 4
PREPARATION TIME: 45 MINUTES
COOKING TIME: 60 MINUTES

A thumb-size piece of ginger
2 scallions
3½ oz (100 g) water chestnuts
3½ oz (100 g) shrimp, peeled and
  deveined (see page 40)
8¾ oz (250 g) white crabmeat
7 oz (200 g) ground pork
Vegetable oil, for frying

The Marinade
½ tsp salt
½ tsp black pepper
1 Tbsp light soy sauce
2 tsp sesame oil
2 Tbsp water
1½ Tbsp cornstarch

The Sauce
A thumb-size piece of ginger, finely sliced
1 Napa cabbage, cut into
  1¼-in (3-cm) squares
1½ Tbsp oyster sauce
1¼ cups (300 ml) chicken broth
A large handful of cilantro, chopped

PREPARATION
- Finely dice the ginger, scallions, water chestnuts, and shrimp and put them in a large bowl. Add the crabmeat, ground pork, and all the marinade ingredients and mix together to form a smooth paste.

- Fill a bowl with cold water. Dip the palms of your hands into the water, then pick up and roll a portion of the meatball mix into ping-pong sized balls. Repeat until all the mix has been used, placing the meatballs on a large cold plate once rolled.

COOKING
- Half-fill a large pot, wok, or deep-fryer with vegetable oil and heat to 350°F (180°C), or until the tip of a wooden chopstick or skewer starts to fizz after a second or so in the oil. Deep-fry the meatballs in batches for 4 minutes until golden brown, then remove from the oil and let drain on paper towels.

- While the meatballs are draining, make the sauce. Heat 1 Tbsp of vegetable oil in a separate saucepan over medium heat. Add the ginger and the Napa cabbage and fry for 2 to 3 minutes, then add the oyster sauce and broth and bring to a boil.

- Reduce the heat to a simmer, carefully lower the meatballs into the sauce, and let cook, covered, for 30 to 40 minutes until the sauce has thickened by half. Spoon the meatballs and sauce into bowls and serve with steamed rice.

! TIP: The traditional way to beat the meatball mix is to use a cupped hand to scoop the mix from the bowl (holding the bowl tight to the work top with the other, clean hand) and then throw it back into the bowl. This not only tenderizes the meat, but will also push any air out of the mix, giving the meatballs a smooth texture.

Ingredients like fermented tofu and eggs provide a great way of thickening sauces without the use of cornstarch. The fermented red tofu used here has an intensely salty flavor if eaten alone, which is very much an acquired taste. However, when it's made into a paste and cooked into this braising liquid, it adds a silky finish to the sauce and gives a real depth of flavor. This dish, a favorite of my dad's, is a family meal we had often—its intense flavor is perfect paired with rice and something light and fresh like a Flash-Fried Morning Glory (see page 144) or Pickled Lotus Root and Spinach (see page 150).

BRAISED PORK BELLY IN FERMENTED TOFU

SERVES: 4
PREPARATION TIME: 30 MINUTES
COOKING TIME: 2 HOURS 15 MINUTES

4 eggs
2 garlic cloves
1 Tbsp vegetable oil
1 x 1¼ lb (600 g) pork belly piece
Approximately 2 cups (450 ml) hot water

The Sauce
1 cube of fermented red tofu, plus
  1 Tbsp fermented tofu liquid
2 Tbsp dark soy sauce
1 Tbsp Chinkiang black rice vinegar
1 Tbsp granulated sugar
1 tsp sesame oil

PREPARATION

- For the sauce, put the fermented tofu and liquid into a small bowl or ramekin and crush it with the base of a teaspoon to form a paste, then mix together with the dark soy sauce, black vinegar, sugar, and sesame oil.

- Hard-boil the eggs and then peel them. Once peeled, cut three small lines vertically into each egg while keeping them whole (this allows the sauce to soak through the eggs while they are braising).

- Mince the garlic and set it aside.

COOKING

- Heat the vegetable oil in a large saucepan over high heat. Add the garlic to the pot and cook, stirring, for 30 seconds until lightly browned. Add the sauce and bring to a boil, then reduce the heat to a simmer.

- Meanwhile, heat a frying pan over medium-high heat. Add the pork belly piece to the pan and sear on all sides, ensuring the skin is well-sealed and golden brown.

- Once seared, add the pork to the saucepan skin-side down and baste well with the sauce. Bring the sauce to a boil and cook, continuing to baste as you do so, for 5 to 6 minutes. The sauce should caramelize, reduce, and cling to the pork during this process.

- Once the sauce is thick and coating the meat well, turn the pork skin-side up and pour over enough hot water to cover it completely. Stir everything together well, cover with a lid, and let simmer over low heat for 1½ hours, turning the pork occasionally, until it is soft, succulent, and full of color.

- Uncover, add the eggs to the braising liquid, and continue simmering for another 30 minutes, turning the eggs every 10 minutes to ensure they absorb the sauce evenly. Arrange on a large platter and serve.

↻ **SWAPSIES:** If you cannot find fermented tofu, make a paste out of one of the hard-boiled egg yolks instead. The texture will thicken the sauce, much like the tofu does, giving the dish its silky finish.

Poaching is such a wonderful way to cook fish. The idea behind poaching in a light and earthy broth like this is to keep the cod fillet soft and delicate, while accentuating the flavor of the fish itself. The carrot and the celery add color, while the wood ear mushroom provides a great contrasting texture to the flaky white fish.

POACHED COD FILLET WITH WOOD EAR MUSHROOM AND SCALLION BROTH

SERVES: 2
PREPARATION TIME: 30 MINUTES
COOKING TIME: 20 MINUTES

A thumb-size piece of ginger
½ carrot
2 scallions
½ stalk celery
2 garlic cloves, skin on
1 x 10½ oz (300 g) cod fillet, descaled, skin on
A handful of dried wood ear mushrooms, soaked and drained (see page 47)
1¼ cups (300 ml) fish or chicken broth
1½ Tbsp vegetable oil
Salt and freshly ground black pepper

The Marinade
1 egg white
½ tsp salt
½ tsp granulated sugar
2 tsp sesame oil
½ Tbsp cornstarch

PREPARATION

- Finely slice the ginger and carrot. Cut the scallions into 1¼-in (3-cm) chunks. Peel off the fibrous parts of the celery, then slice it into 1¼-in (3-cm) chunks.

- Using the flat side of a knife or cleaver, smash the garlic to release its flavor, but do not peel or discard the skin.

- Slice the cod fillet diagonally into ⅜-in (1-cm) thick slices and put it in a bowl. Add the marinade ingredients and, using your hands, gently massage them into the fish pieces until they are well coated.

✱ **BUILD YOUR WOK CLOCK:** place the garlic at 12 o'clock, then arrange the ginger, scallion, carrot, celery, mushrooms, broth, and fish bowl clockwise around your plate.

COOKING

- Heat the vegetable oil in a wok over low heat, add the garlic cloves in their skins, and cook for 4 to 5 minutes, turning occasionally, until the skins start to brown.

- Increase the heat to medium-high, add the ginger and scallion to the wok, and stir-fry for 1 minute until fragrant and lightly browned. Add the carrot, celery, and mushrooms to the wok and stir-fry for another 2 to 3 minutes.

- Pour the broth into the wok and bring to a vigorous boil, then carefully add the fish pieces, reduce the heat to a medium simmer, and cook for another 3 minutes, until the fish pieces are white and opaque all the way through. Season with salt and pepper to taste and serve with steamed rice.

❗ **TIP:** Keeping the skin on the garlic in this recipe helps protect it from burning in the pan, while the slow cooking allows its flavors to infuse slowly into the oil. Minced garlic would burn very quickly if cooked this way.

I first tried this dish when I was ten years old at a stall in a hawker center in Singapore, not Hainan. One mouthful transformed me from being a picky eater to an adventurous and engaged one like the rest of my family. The thing about Singapore's hawker centers is that each stall specializes in just one dish and does it well. If you find the right stand—often the one with the longest queue—you will know instantaneously. Cooked well, this dish is sure to make anyone's mouth water.

POACHED HAINANESE CHICKEN RICE WITH GINGER OIL

SERVES: 6
PREPARATION TIME: 10 MINUTES
COOKING TIME: 1 HOUR 30 MINUTES

1 x 3¼ lb (1.5 kg) chicken
½ tsp salt
A thumb-size piece of ginger
1 chicken bouillon cube
1 garlic clove, smashed
2 Tbsp sesame oil
3 Tbsp light soy sauce
Scant 1¼ cups (250 g) Thai fragrant
  jasmine rice

Ginger Oil
A large piece of ginger, minced
3 scallions, minced
¼ tsp salt
2 Tbsp vegetable oil

PREPARATION

- Find the parson's nose of your chicken (it's at the rear end and resembles something of a triangular tail no larger than the joint of your thumb) and cut it off—it will make your broth bitter if not discarded.

- Rub the chicken all over with the salt, then place it in a large saucepan and cover it with cold water until fully submerged. Finely slice the ginger and add three-quarters of it to the pan along with the bouillon cube.

- Using the flat side of a knife or cleaver, smash the garlic and peel away the skin. Set aside with the remaining ginger. Mix the sesame oil and light soy sauce together in a small bowl.

COOKING

- Cover the saucepan with a lid and bring to a boil. Once the water starts to boil, reduce the heat and let simmer, covered, for 20 minutes. Remove the saucepan from the heat and let the chicken sit in the covered pot for another 40 minutes.

- Carefully remove the chicken from the pan, setting aside the cooking liquid, and submerge it in a separate pot of cold water for 2 minutes. Drain and then baste it in the sesame and soy mix. Set aside to rest for 20 minutes.

- Meanwhile, wash the rice, then place in a pan with the remaining ginger, the garlic clove, and 1⅓ cups (320 ml) of the chicken poaching liquid. Mix together well, then cover with a lid and bring to a boil on high heat. Once boiling, lower the heat to a simmer and cook for 10 minutes, then turn the heat off and let steam with the lid on for another 15 minutes.

- While the rice is steaming, make the ginger oil. Add the minced ginger, scallions, and salt to a small serving bowl and mix together. Heat the oil in a small frying pan until smoking-hot, then pour over the ginger and scallion to sizzle. Mix together well.

- Carve the chicken and arrange on a large serving platter with the ginger oil and chicken rice. Accompany with slices of skinless cucumber and chili sauce, if desired.

- **! TIP:** To check that the chicken is thoroughly cooked after sitting in the hot water for 40 minutes, poke a small, sharp paring knife through the thickest part of the thigh and press into the skin a little. If the juices run clear and no blood is present, the chicken is ready to eat.

Imagine getting all your friends together for a dinner party and having no space left on the table once the food is out for even a pair of chopsticks and a bowl. An eating event of grand proportions, Steamboat is as exciting as it sounds, yet the concept itself is actually quite simple: one or two poaching broths, bubbling away in the middle of the table, surrounded by fresh seafood, meat, and vegetables with numerous condiments and minced herbs and spices on the side to make your own dipping sauces. What a way to eat!

STEAMBOAT

SERVES: 8 TO 10
PREPARATION TIME: 5 HOURS
COOKING TIME: UP TO YOU!

1¾ to 2¼ lb (800 g to 1 kg) fine slices of meat such as rib-eye or lamb steaks
1¾ to 2¼ lb (800 g to 1 kg) fish fillet slices
1¾ to 2¼ lb (800 g to 1 kg) shellfish
A variety of Chinese vegetables such as bok choy, choi sum, and kai choi
A variety of noodles
A selection of finely sliced herbs and chiles
A selection of Chinese dipping sauces

Roasted Pork Bone Broth
1 lb 2 oz (500 g) pork bones
5 garlic cloves
A thumb-size piece of ginger, sliced
3 large onions
2 onions
1 celery stalk
5 scallions
10 dried shiitake mushrooms

Mushroom Broth
5 garlic cloves
A thumb-size piece of ginger
3 large onions
2 onions
1 celery stalk
5 scallions
10 dried shiitake mushrooms
14 oz (400 g) dried yellow soybeans

PREPARATION

• Preheat the oven to 450°F (230°C).

• For the pork bone broth, arrange the bones on a large roasting tray and roast in the oven for 40 minutes, then tip into a large saucepan or stockpot with all the other ingredients and cover with cold water. Bring to a boil, then reduce the heat to a simmer and cook for 4 to 5 hours.

• Meanwhile make the mushroom broth. Put all the ingredients in another large saucepan or stockpot and cover with cold water. Bring to a boil, then reduce the heat to a simmer and cook for 4 to 5 hours.

• When both your broths are ready, transfer them into steamboat pots and bring them (or your alternative setup, see Tip) to the table.

• Arrange your chosen meats, fish, shellfish, vegetables, and noodles in bowls or on plates around the table —meat should be placed on one side of the table, separate to the fish and shellfish. Arrange a selection of cooking chopsticks or tongs, serving bowls, bowls of fresh herbs and chiles, and a selection of your favorite Chinese sauces around the table.

COOKING

• Light the steamboats and bring them to a gentle simmer. Using chopsticks or tongs, lower your chosen ingredient into one of the hot broths and poach until cooked to your liking. All meat and seafood should be poached for a minimum of 4 to 5 minutes to cook through thoroughly.

• Remove your ingredient from the broth and cover with your favorite dipping sauce, then eat, enjoy, and repeat.

❗ TIP: Steamboat pots and lighters, along with specific cooking utensils for steamboat cooking such as mini cooking baskets, can be found in Chinese grocery stores, though if you have a couple of camping stoves or portable induction stoves, these can work in a similar fashion. Ready-cut slices of meat and fish specifically for steamboats can also be found in most Chinese grocery stores.

ROASTING AND DOUBLE-COOKING

While roasting and double-cooking play big parts in Chinese cuisine, because of their time-consuming nature these techniques can feel overwhelming or intimidating to some. This chapter is my ultimate tribute to the slow-cooking process—the recipes it contains are not necessarily difficult, but require a certain amount of loving patience that doesn't always align well with the day-to-day bustle of modern life. These are recipes to be tackled on a quiet weekend, and the results are worth waiting for.

While traditional Chinese roasting ovens are hard to come by these days, in the old days a restaurant would have a large walk-in clay oven. This would have a huge chimney in the middle of its roof and small wind tunnels built into the walls to allow air to circulate through the oven itself—the thick clay walls would hold in the heat while the meat would be hung along the inside walls, with coal pits underneath creating the heat for the slow-cooked, "wind-dried" style of cooking. This inventive way of cooking allowed the outside skin of the meat to char away while the meat would slowly roast until succulent and tender, creating a crispy skin and melt-in-the-mouth meat. These days restaurants use commercial stainless-steel ovens that do a very similar job and, though it can be difficult to replicate such a unique cooking environment at home, there are ways and means of creating similar outcomes with a domestic oven.

Double-cooking is precisely what it describes: when two or more of any of the basic techniques learned here in the book are combined to cook one dish. As a balance of textures is so important in Chinese food, the Chinese love to use double-cooking processes to give different textures to meat, seafood, and even certain vegetable dishes. There are no specific rules with double-cooking, though there are some general guidelines as to how to order the cooking techniques to ensure a successful outcome (blanching, poaching, deep-frying, or braising tend to come first, while the second or third processes are more likely to be roasting, stir-frying, or steaming). Sometimes a dish may use up to four or five different cooking techniques; the typical dim sum dish of chickens' feet is a good example, where, in order to give the skin its signature melt-in-the-mouth feel, the feet are blanched, then dried, then deep-fried, then braised, then marinated, and finally steamed to finish. This may seem a little excessive, but it's an amazing way to make something so seemingly tasteless take in so much flavor. There is indeed method in the madness!

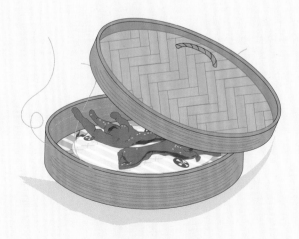

This classic Cantonese dish is often made using a filling of dace, a paste of small fish that can be bought in the local markets already made up, seasoned, and ready to use. Unfortunately, it is not easy to find this luxury outside of Canton, so to mimic the paste's texture I like to use a combination of blended shrimp and fish—the fish providing the softness, while the shrimp gives it the bite. With a speedily whipped together sauce poured over the top, this roasted vegetable dish makes for a great quick and easy dinner.

SEAFOOD-STUFFED ROAST PEPPERS AND EGGPLANTS

SERVES: 4
PREPARATION TIME: 25 MINUTES
COOKING TIME: 20 MINUTES

3½ oz (100 g) cod fillet or other white fish
   fillet, skin off
7 oz (200 g) raw shrimp, peeled and
   deveined (see page 40)
A pinch of salt
A pinch of black pepper
2 scallions
A large handful of cilantro, plus extra
   to garnish
1 garlic clove
1 large eggplant
2 red bell peppers
3 Tbsp cornstarch
3 Tbsp vegetable oil

The Sauce
1 Tbsp oyster sauce
½ Tbsp light soy sauce
½ tsp granulated sugar
⅝ cup (150 ml) chicken broth
A thumb-size piece of ginger

PREPARATION

- Preheat the oven to 400°F (200°C). Mix together all the sauce ingredients except the ginger in a bowl and set aside.

- Cut the fish fillet into coarse pieces before placing in a food processor along with the shrimp. Blend together gradually, adding a large pinch each of salt and pepper as you go, until a thick paste forms.

- Mince the scallions, cilantro, and garlic and put in a mixing bowl along with the fish and shrimp paste. Mix everything together well.

- Cut the eggplant diagonally into 1¼-in (3-cm) thick slices, then slice each piece through the skin three-quarters of the way through without cutting the pieces in two (this will effectively make a sandwich, with a pocket for the filling). Place the eggplant pieces in a large bowl filled with salted water and set aside.

- Cut the peppers into large wedges leaving the inside membranes intact (they will help to keep the filling in). Dust the inside of each vegetable piece with the cornstarch, then stuff each piece with the fish mixture. Once all the vegetable pieces have been filled, pour over 2 Tbsp of the vegetable oil, turning the pieces in it to ensure they are all well coated.

COOKING

- Arrange the peppers filling-side up on a baking sheet along with the eggplant pieces and roast them in the oven for 20 minutes until the filling has become lightly browned and the shrimp are coral pink in color.

- Five minutes before serving, heat the remaining 1 Tbsp of oil over medium heat in a saucepan or wok. Add the ginger and fry for 30 seconds until fragrant, then add the sauce mixture and bring to a boil. Boil for 3 to 5 minutes, or until reduced by half, then pour over the stuffed vegetables and sprinkle over some chopped cilantro to finish. Serve.

! TIP: This seafood mixture works really well as a stuffing for other vegetables such as zucchini or marrows, or even large chiles (just be sure to take the seeds out before stuffing unless you like things ferociously hot!).

I once had a customer who really tested my knowledge. It seemed he cooked Chinese food at home more times in a week than I did, yet he still wanted to come for lessons. He was such an enthusiast he even went as far as hanging a whole duck in his closet overnight, in with the clean bath towels and all. Needless to say his wife was not so enthusiastic! This recipe, a simplified version of the classic Cantonese roast duck and rice, is a great way to try something new—without ruining your clothes, towels, or marriage …

CANTONESE ROAST DUCK LEGS

SERVES: 2
PREPARATION TIME: 15 MINUTES PLUS MARINATING
COOKING TIME: 40 MINUTES

2 duck leg and thigh joints

The Marinade
A thumb-size piece of ginger
1 scallionn
4 Tbsp honey
4 Tbsp red rice vinegar or
  red wine vinegar
1 Tbsp oyster sauce
½ Tbsp hoisin sauce
2 Tbsp Shaoxing rice wine
½ tsp Chinese five-spice

PREPARATION

- Finely slice the ginger and scallion and place in a bowl along with the rest of the marinade ingredients. Mix together well.

- Bring a saucepan of water to a boil, add the duck legs, and blanch for 3 minutes. Remove from the pan and cool under cold running water, then drain and add to the marinade. Using your hands, massage the marinade into the duck pieces until evenly coated. Cover the bowl with plastic wrap, transfer to the refrigerator, and let marinate overnight.

COOKING

- Preheat the oven to 325°F (160°C).

- Spoon the ginger and scallion pieces from the marinade (setting aside the liquid in the bowl) onto the bottom of a roasting tray and place the duck legs on top. Roast in the oven for 40 minutes, basting the legs with the reserved marinade every 10 minutes with a brush, until the skin is nicely caramelized.

- Using a large, sharp knife or chopper, cut the duck legs into ¾-in (2-cm) thick pieces through the bone (see Tip), and place on top of a bed of steamed jasmine rice. Serve with Glazed Chinese Greens (see page 147).

! **TIP:** When chopping through the bones of the duck legs, slice through the meat first, until you hit the bone. Now give the top of your cleaver or knife a good hit with either your palm or a rolling pin to cut through the bone cleanly. This way will mean you don't have apply too much pressure with your bare hands and won't end up hacking away at the meat.

If there's one dish that brings together my extended family, it's crispy pork. A celebration doesn't feel right without it—so much so that a roast pig has made an appearance at the last two consecutive Pang weddings. In the last few days of my father's life he could barely even string a sentence together, yet he still managed to request a meal of crispy pork and rice, and smiled at the thought of it. And so this book would not be complete without it. The blanching process and initial slow cooking here will help to get rid of the many solid impurities and excess fat that pork seems to hold in its skin while also softening the meat.

CRISPY PORK BELLY

SERVES: 4
PREPARATION TIME: 15 MINUTES
COOKING TIME: 3 HOURS

1 x 1 lb 2 oz (500 g) pork belly piece
2 tsp salt
1 to 2 tsp Chinese five-spice

PREPARATION

- Place the pork belly piece skin-side down in a large saucepan and cover with boiling water. Bring to a boil, then reduce to a simmer and cook for 5 minutes before removing the meat from the pan. (Some scum may form on the top of the water; it is just some of the impurities and excess fat the pork holds within its skin and will be discarded once the pork is blanched.)

- Remove the meat from the pan and run under cold water to cool. Once cool, pat the skin dry with paper towels and score gently using the tip of a sharp knife in diagonal "crisscross" cuts along the top of the skin, trying to only open up the fat and not cut into the meat itself.

- Dry the skin with paper towels once more and rub the salt into it. Rub the five-spice onto the sides and bottom of the meat only, not the skin.

COOKING

- Preheat the oven to 265°F (130°C). Place the pork on a wire rack above a roasting pan skin-side up and roast in the oven for 1½ hours. Now turn the oven up to 450°F (230°C) and roast for another 30 to 45 minutes, or until the skin is golden brown and crispy all the way through. To judge whether the pork skin is crispy enough, give it a flick with your finger; if the sound is hollow like that from the bottom of a well-baked loaf of bread, then the pork is definitely crispy enough.

- Remove the pork from the oven and let rest for 15 minutes. Turn the pork skin-side down on a cutting board and slice through the skin with a sharp large knife or cleaver, pressing down on the top of the blade to slice through the crackling. Serve.

! **TIP:** If you do not have a fan function on your oven, let the pork out dry in a cool, dry area of your kitchen for 1 hour before placing in the oven.

The double-cooking process here for the beans may seem like a lot of effort, but it will leave them soft and succulent and is well worth it. The traditional way to cook this dish is actually to deep-fry the beans first, before flash-frying and then tossing them into the slightly sweet, slightly spicy sauce. However, on the home front, I find it a bit too much to use 4½ cups (1 L) of oil just for a bag of beans and I do think the dish comes out just as well blanching them in hot water rather than hot oil.

STIR-FRIED GREEN BEANS WITH CHILI HOISIN

SERVES: 2 AS A MAIN OR 4 AS A SIDE
PREPARATION TIME: 10 MINUTES
COOKING TIME: 10 MINUTES

8¾ oz (250 g) fine green beans
½ onion
A small piece of ginger
1 fresh Thai chile
2 garlic cloves
1 Tbsp vegetable oil

Chili Hoisin
1 tsp Chiu Chow chili oil
1 Tbsp hoisin sauce
1 Tbsp Shaoxing rice wine
A dash of dark soy sauce

PREPARATION

- Trim the beans and drop them into a pan of boiling water. Blanch them for 2 minutes, then drain and cool under cold running water.

- Finely slice the onion and ginger. Dice the Thai chile. Using the flat side of a knife or cleaver, smash the garlic cloves to release their flavor and remove the skin.

- Mix the chili hoisin ingredients together in a small bowl or ramekin.

- ❋ **BUILD YOUR WOK CLOCK:** place your finely sliced onion at 12 o'clock, then arrange the ginger, garlic, blanched green beans, chile, chili hoisin, and sauce bowl clockwise around your plate.

COOKING

- Heat the vegetable oil in a wok until smoking-hot. Add the onion and stir-fry for 30 seconds until slightly softened, then add the ginger and garlic and stir-fry for another 30 seconds.

- Keeping the heat as high a heat as possible, add the blanched green beans and stir-fry for 1 to 2 minutes until the beans have "blistered" around the edges. Add the chile and chili hoisin, bring to a vigorous boil, and continue to cook, stirring, for another 1 to 2 minutes until the sauce has reduced and is just coating the beans.

- Remove from the heat and spoon into a large bowl. Serve.

- ❗ **TIP:** The spiciness of the green beans balances very well with something delicate like the Whole Steamed Gurnard with Ginger and Scallions (see page 96). Add a bowl of steamed jasmine rice to make a lovely simple dinner for three or four people.

In many parts of China and Hong Kong, cuttlefish are actually more popular than squid and, as cuttlefish have much thicker meat than squid, the double-cooking process detailed here is essential. I find that large squid also benefit from this prepoaching—it softens the squid significantly, allowing the pieces to take in more flavor when stir-fried in the savory sauce.

TWICE-COOKED SQUID WITH GARLIC AND GREEN CHILE

SERVES: 4
PREPARATION TIME: 1 HOUR
COOKING TIME: 10 MINUTES

1 lb 2 oz (500 g) squid, cleaned and quills removed (get your fish supplier to do this for you)
1 Tbsp cornstarch
1 tsp preserved black beans
3 garlic cloves
A small piece of ginger
A pinch of salt
3 scallions, plus extra to garnish
1 red onion
2 large fresh green chiles
2 Tbsp vegetable oil

The Sauce
½ Tbsp light soy sauce
2 Tbsp oyster sauce
2 Tbsp Shaoxing rice wine
1 tsp sesame oil
½ tsp granulated sugar

PREPARATION

- Wash the squid tubes and slice them open to lay them flat. Run the tip of your knife along the squid pieces in a diagonal crisscross pattern (this will help the squid curl up nicely when cooking).

- Add the prepared squid to a pan of boiling water, reduce the heat to a simmer, and cook over low heat for 45 minutes. Remove the squid from the water with a slotted spoon and cool under cold running water, then drain and place in a bowl with the cornstarch and mix together well.

- Give the black beans a quick rinse under cold water, then tip them into a small bowl. Mince the garlic and ginger and add them to the black beans with a pinch of salt. Lightly crush the ingredients together with the back of a teaspoon.

- Cut the scallions into coarse chunks and the red onion and green chiles into ⅜-in (1-cm) dice. Mix the sauce ingredients together in a small bowl.

- ❋ BUILD YOUR WOK CLOCK: place the diced red onion at 12 o'clock, then arrange the scallions, garlic and bean mixture, chiles, squid, and sauce bowl clockwise around the plate.

COOKING

- Heat 1 Tbsp of vegetable oil in a wok over high heat until smoking-hot, then add the onion and cook for 1 minute until slightly softened.

- Add the scallions and bean mixture and stir-fry for another 30 seconds, then add the green chiles and fry for 30 seconds more, maintaining high heat all the time. Transfer the vegetables to a bowl.

- Add the remaining 1 Tbsp of oil to the wok and bring it back to high heat. Once smoking-hot, add the squid and flash-fry for 30 seconds to sear the squid all over. Return the vegetables to the wok, pour over the sauce, and bring to a vigorous boil. Cook for 1 to 2 minutes until the sauce has reduced and thickened slightly and is just coating the squid and vegetables.

- Serve with freshly sliced scallion to garnish.

Cooking a dish like this perfectly is a little step up from just deep-frying some shrimp and throwing a sauce on top. The deep-fry at the beginning of this double-cooking process acts as a gentle blanch in hot oil that seals the shrimp lightly, allowing the sauce to seep through the air pockets within the meat and shells and leaving a sensational flavor on your palate.

TWICE-COOKED SAMBAL TIGER SHRIMP

SERVES: 4
PREPARATION TIME: 20 MINUTES
COOKING TIME: 10 MINUTES

10 Thai shallots, peeled
A thumb-size piece of ginger
A large handful of cilantro
1 medium tomato
5 dried red chiles
1 lb 2 oz (500 g) uncooked large tiger
  shrimp, shells on and deveined (see
  page 40)
2 Tbsp cornstarch
Sea salt and freshly ground black pepper
Vegetable oil, for frying

The Sauce
1 Tbsp sambal sauce or
  sambal paste
2 Tbsp dark soy sauce
1 Tbsp granulated sugar
1 Tbsp rice vinegar
7 Tbsp (100 ml) chicken or fish broth

PREPARATION

- Finely slice the Thai shallots and ginger. Coarsely chop the cilantro. Cut the tomato into eighths.

- Put the dried red chiles in a small bowl, cover with hot water, and let soak for 5 minutes, then drain and coarsely chop.

- Mix the sauce ingredients together in another small bowl.

- Butterfly the shrimp, keeping the shells intact by cutting a line from underneath the head of the shrimp to the tip of the tail using a sharp knife or scissors and opening up the shrimp fully. Put the shrimp in a bowl, cover with the cornstarch, and season with salt and pepper. Mix together thoroughly.

✿ **BUILD YOUR WOK CLOCK:** place your finely sliced shallots at 12 o'clock, then arrange the ginger, red chiles, tomatoes, sauce bowl, shrimp, and cilantro clockwise around your plate.

COOKING

- Half-fill a large pot, wok, or deep-fryer with vegetable oil and heat to 325°F (165°C), or until the tip of a wooden chopstick or skewer starts to bubble (but not fizz) after 2 to 3 seconds in the oil. Carefully add the shrimp and deep-fry for 2 to 3 minutes until the shrimp are a light coral and the shells are slightly browned. Remove the shrimp from the oil and drain well on paper towels.

- Heat 1 Tbsp of vegetable oil in a wok until smoking. Add the shallots and ginger and stir-fry for 1 minute until slightly softened and fragrant. Add the red chiles and tomatoes and stir-fry for another 30 seconds.

- Keeping the heat as high as possible, pour the sauce into the wok and bring to a vigorous boil. Add the shrimp, reduce the heat to a simmer, and cook for 2 minutes until the sauce has thickened and forms a coating around the shrimp.

- Remove from the heat and sprinkle over the cilantro to finish. Serve.

❗ **TIP:** Peeling Thai shallots can be quite cumbersome. To make life easier, simply soak the shallots in hot water for 2 to 3 minutes, then cut them in half and peel off the outer layer.

This succulent yet crisp pork belly is a great recipe for a special occasion—just braise and cool the meat the day before you want to serve it, leaving you very little to do on the day itself. The flavors added to the poaching liquid bring a subtle depth of flavor to the stir-fry, while the initial poaching will also extract the fatty impurities from the meat, making it taste much healthier.

TWICE-COOKED CHILI PORK

SERVES: 4
PREPARATION TIME: 2 HOURS 30 MINUTES
COOKING TIME: 15 MINUTES

1 x 10½ oz (300 g) pork belly piece
2 star anise
1 cinnamon stick
2 cloves
5 black peppercorns
A small piece of ginger
2 garlic cloves
1 onion
2 large red chiles
A small handful of cilantro
2 Tbsp vegetable oil

The Marinade
2 tsp sesame oil
¼ tsp salt
¼ tsp black pepper
2 tsp cornstarch

The Sauce
½ Tbsp hoisin sauce
½ Tbsp rice wine
½ Tbsp Chinkiang black rice vinegar
1 tsp chili bean sauce
1 tsp chilli oil
A dash of dark soy sauce

PREPARATION

- To poach the pork, place the pork belly in a medium saucepan along with the star anise, cinnamon, cloves, and black peppercorns. Cover with hot water, bring to a simmer, and poach for at least 45 minutes (for best results, poach for up to 2 hours). Remove the meat from the pan, discarding the poaching liquid, and run under cold water to cool. Once cool, pat the skin dry with paper towels, then place on a plate, cover with plastic wrap, and let chill in the refrigerator for a minimum of 1 hour, preferably overnight.

- When you are ready to cook, remove the pork from the refrigerator and slice it into thin pieces. Place the pieces in a mixing bowl, add the marinade ingredients, and let marinate for 20 minutes.

- Finely slice the ginger and garlic. Slice the onion into thin strips. Dice the chiles and coarsely chop the cilantro. Mix the sauce ingredients together in a small bowl or ramekin.

- ✸ **BUILD YOUR WOK CLOCK:** Place your onions at 12 o'clock, then arrange the ginger, garlic, chile, meat bowl, sauce bowl, and cilantro clockwise around the plate.

COOKING

- Heat 1 Tbsp of vegetable oil in a wok over high heat until smoking. Add the onion and cook for 1 minute until slightly softened, then add the ginger, garlic, and chiles and cook for another minute until fragrant and smoky.

- Push the vegetables to the back of your wok, add the remaining 1 Tbsp of vegetable oil, and return to smoking point before adding the pork slices. Spread them out in one layer and let sear for 1 minute until browned, then turn the pork slices over and repeat on the other side.

- Spoon the veg over the top of the pork and pour over the sauce ingredients. Bring to a vigorous boil and stir-fry for 2 to 3 minutes until the sauce has thickened and coats the meat nicely. Spoon onto a serving plate and sprinkle over the cilantro to finish.

- ❗ **TIP:** The long cooling period will help to tighten the meat up and allow any soft fats to solidify once again, making it much easier to slice the next day.

Certain meats like chicken wings or pork belly are quite difficult to cook quickly from raw on a broiler or barbecue as the fatty skin tends to catch and burn much sooner than the meat itself takes to cook. Braising the chicken wings first helps to break down the waxiness of the skin and packs the flavor of the braising liquid into the meat, while cooking it through thoroughly. Cooking your chicken wings this way gives them a perfect chargrilled finish that makes them irresistibly moreish.

CHILI AND PLUM SAUCE WINGS

SERVES: 4
PREPARATION TIME: 10 MINUTES
COOKING TIME: 40 MINUTES

A thumb-size piece of ginger
1 garlic clove, finely diced
1 large red chile, finely diced
10½ oz (300 g) chicken wings
¼ tsp Chinese five-spice
1 Tbsp vegetable oil
Approximately 1¼ cups (300 ml) water
A small handful of cilantro sprigs,
  to garnish

The Sauce
4 Tbsp plum sauce
1 tsp chili bean sauce
A dash of dark soy sauce

PREPARATION
- Slice the ginger into fine matchsticks. Finely dice the garlic and chile.

- Mix the sauce ingredients together in a small bowl or ramekin.

✳ **BUILD YOUR WOK CLOCK:** place your chicken wings at 12 o'clock, then arrange the five-spice, ginger, garlic, chile, sauce bowl, and cilantro clockwise around the plate.

COOKING
- Heat the vegetable oil in a medium saucepan over medium heat. Add the chicken wings and cook, turning, for 2 to 3 minutes until browned on all sides.

- Add the five-spice, ginger, garlic, and chile and cook, stirring, for another minute, then pour over the sauce ingredients and bring to a boil. Cook for 3 to 5 minutes, stirring, until the sauce has reduced and is coating the chicken wings. Add enough hot water just to cover the chicken pieces, bring to a simmer, and cook, covered, for 15 to 20 minutes over low heat until the chicken is cooked through but the skin is still intact. Transfer the wings onto a roasting tray using a slotted spoon, setting aside the sauce for basting.

- Finish the wings off on a hot barbecue or put under a hot broiler for 3 to 5 minutes, basting with excess sauce every minute or so, until they are lightly charred and caramelized. Serve garnished with a few cilantro sprigs.

↻ **SWAPSIE:** You can swap out the wings for chicken thighs and legs and follow the same cooking process—just be sure to braise thicker pieces of meat for at least 25 minutes to ensure they are properly cooked through.

Here is my take on a simple duck and pancake recipe that brings together double-cooking and roasting techniques from both Chinese and Western backgrounds. I like the duck breast medium rare; however the skin should be as crispy as possible. This is why the initial blanching is necessary—dissolving the skin's outer layer enables it to become crispier when fried and roasted. The cucumber pickle and spicy plum sauce are great alternatives to the classic hoisin, cucumber, and scallion combination and give the dish a lovely, gentle touch.

CRISPY DUCK BREAST WITH PANCAKES AND CUCUMBER PICKLE

SERVES: 4
PREPARATION TIME: 30 MINUTES
COOKING TIME: 30 MINUTES

2 large duck breasts
½ tsp salt
¼ tsp Chinese five-spice
16 to 20 duck pancakes

Cucumber Pickle
1 scallion
½ cucumber
2 Tbsp Chinkiang black
   rice vinegar
2 Tbsp granulated sugar
¼ tsp salt
½ Tbsp light soy sauce
1 Tbsp hot water
8 crushed Sichuan peppercorns
1 garlic clove, finely sliced

Spicy Plum Dipping Sauce
2 tsp chili garlic sauce
4 tsp plum sauce
A dash of dark soy sauce
2 Tbsp cold water

PREPARATION

- For the cucumber pickle, slice the scallion and cucumber into fine matchsticks and place in a bowl. Add the remaining ingredients and mix together well.

- Mix the spicy plum dipping sauce ingredients together in a separate small bowl or ramekin.

- Place the duck breast in a saucepan and cover with boiling water. Bring to a boil and blanch for 2 to 3 minutes before removing from the pan and running under cold water to cool. Once cool, pat the skin dry with paper towels and score using the tip of a sharp knife in diagonal cuts along the top of the skin, trying only to open up the fat and not cut into the meat itself.

- Rub the salt into the duck breast and then dab the skin dry with paper towels. Rub the five-spice onto the sides and bottom of the meat only, not the skin. Dab the skin dry once more to remove any extra moisture.

COOKING

- Preheat the oven to 400°F (200°C).

- Place the duck breast skin-side down in a cold frying pan and let the pan heat up to medium-high heat, frying the duck for 6 to 8 minutes, or until the skin is golden brown. Press down on the sides during the frying process to ensure all parts of the skin become crispy.

- Place the duck breast skin-side up on a wire rack above a roasting pan and roast in the oven for 6 to 8 minutes to your liking (see Tip). Remove from the oven and let rest for 5 minutes.

- While the duck breast is resting, steam the pancakes. Place a bamboo steamer over a wok a third filled with boiling water. Arrange the pancakes in the steamer and steam for 3 to 5 minutes.

- Cut the duck into thin slices and serve with the pickle and dipping sauce, accompanied by the pancakes in the steamer.

- **! TIP:** To check whether the duck breast is cooked through to your liking, press it with your fingertips. If the resistance is the same as when you push your fingertips into your chin, then the duck is medium. For rare, it should be the same as pushing into your cheek, while well done will offer the same resistance as pressing against your forehead.

These delicious little nuggets never fail to bring in a crowd. They're sweet, sticky, and tender, cheap to make, and simple to prepare, yet guaranteed to be a showstopper at any dinner party or barbecue. They do, however, require a long, slow cook—2 to 3 hours ideally—to ensure that the meat is succulent and falling off the bone, so make sure to plan ahead.

BARBECUED HOISIN AND COLA RIBS

SERVES: 6 TO 8
PREPARATION TIME: 10 MINUTES
COOKING TIME: 3 HOURS 30 MINUTES

4 garlic cloves
A large piece of ginger
30 spare ribs
8 Tbsp tomato ketchup
8 Tbsp hoisin sauce
4 Tbsp granulated sugar
4 Tbsp dark soy sauce
4 Tbsp rice vinegar
2 Tbsp vegetable oil
Generous 2 cups to 4½ cups
   (500 ml to 1 L) cola or cider
½ scallion, minced, to garnish

PREPARATION

- Preheat the oven to 300°F (150°C).

- Mince the garlic and ginger and put in a deep roasting tray or big pot suitable for the oven along with the ribs and all the other ingredients. Mix everything together thoroughly, ensuring the ribs are well covered.

COOKING

- Transfer the ribs to the oven and cook uncovered for at least 2 to 3 hours, basting and turning the ribs every so often so they don't burn (if they do start to "catch," turn your oven down slightly). Toward the end of the cooking time the ribs will start to break up and fall apart slightly—this is a good sign, but you want to keep them as whole as possible (ready for grilling), so be careful when turning.

- Transfer the ribs to a hot barbecue and cook in batches for 2 to 3 minutes on each side until the outsides of the ribs are glazed and charred. Drizzle over a little of the remaining sauce and sprinkle over some minced scallion to garnish. Enjoy.

- **!** **TIP:** If you fancy cooking these on a normal night in (or the weather isn't looking good) then pop the ribs under the hot broiler in the oven instead of on the barbecue after roasting. Although the ribs are always better after they've been grilled slightly, if you just can't wait they can always be eaten straight after roasting in the oven.

SALADS, PICKLES, AND SUGGESTED SIDES

As I mentioned at the very beginning of this book, trying to find the right balance in flavor, texture, and color is, for me, one of the most important things to learn about cooking and eating Chinese food. No good Chinese meal, no matter how delicious, rich, or flavorful, is complete without a side vegetable or pickle to balance out the concentrated flavors of the deep-fried meats, slippery noodles, and stir-fried rich seafood.

Pickling has been a significant form of food preservation all over China since prerefrigeration days, as it has been across many cultures. Though no longer essential, it still deserves its place at the dinner table as well as here in this book. Over the next few pages you will find some simple pickles to go on the side of any meal you decide to cook from this book, all of which can be eaten after just 45 to 60 minutes of pickling.

The quick vegetable sides dishes here also provide a fresh finish to any meal. Serve them with your main course and some steamed rice and you will feel like you are eating in a family home in Hong Kong or China in no time! The most important thing to note when cooking your vegetables is to try not to overcook them. Opposite is a general guide for cooking the most commonly found Chinese greens, whether you are stir-frying, blanching, or steaming them.

VEGETABLE COOKING TIMES

MORNING GLORY (TUNG CHOI)
1 to 2 minutes

BOK CHOY
3 minutes

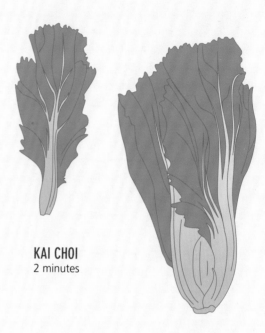

KAI CHOI
2 minutes

CHOI SUM
4 minutes

KAI LAN (CHINESE BROCCOLI)
5 minutes

While visiting Thailand a few years ago I suffered serious wok envy. My wife and I had been commissioned to write a travel book in Phuket and had stumbled across a market in the old town offering all types of mouthwatering Chinese and Thai street treats. There was one old Chinese man cooking by a fierce wok burner who stood out from the rest—you could barely see what he was doing through the flames, but his wok work was absolutely mesmerizing. We ordered a plate of the vegetables, and it was amazing how he made something so simple taste so good.

FLASH-FRIED MORNING GLORY

SERVES: 2
PREPARATION TIME: 10 MINUTES
COOKING TIME: 2 MINUTES

8¾ oz (250 g) morning glory
A thumb-size piece of ginger
3 garlic cloves
2 fresh Thai chiles
1 Tbsp oyster sauce
½ Tbsp light soy sauce
1 Tbsp Shaoxing rice wine
1 tsp sesame oil
2 Tbsp vegetable oil

PREPARATION

- Chop the morning glory stalks into approximately 2-in (5-cm) lengths and place them in a large bowl along with all the leaves.

- Finely slice the ginger. Squash the garlic with the flat side of a knife or cleaver and remove the skin. Using the tip of a sharp knife, pierce the chiles several times, being sure to keep them whole and the stems intact. (This will release a bit of the chile heat and flavor, without making everything overwhelmingly spicy).

- Add the prepared ginger, garlic, and chiles to the bowl along with the sauces, rice wine, and sesame oil.

COOKING

- Heat the vegetable oil in a wok over high heat until smoking-hot.

- Add the vegetable mixture to the wok and stir-fry for 1 to 2 minutes, until the morning glory is tender but still retains its shape and vibrant color. Serve.

! TIP: Be careful not to overcook this dish! So long as it is piping hot and has a good glaze to its outer stem, the morning glory is ready to eat. The whole stalk and all the leaves are edible, so be sure to use every part of the morning glory when flash-frying.

When you order in a Cantonese restaurant, if you are speaking to the waiters in Chinese, the first thing they will ask is what type of tea you would like—reeling off a huge list so quickly that you most probably won't understand, even if you are Chinese yourself! After this, they will do the same for the types of fresh green vegetables that they have in that day, and once you have picked, they will ask you, "With garlic, or oyster sauce?" If they ever have pea shoots in, try them with garlic—they are best eaten this way and are one of my favorite vegetables.

STIR-FRIED PEA SHOOTS WITH GARLIC

SERVES: 2
PREPARATION TIME: 5 MINUTES
COOKING TIME: 3 MINUTES

2 handfuls of pea shoots
2 garlic cloves
1 Tbsp vegetable oil

The Sauce
1 Tbsp Shaoxing rice wine
7 Tbsp (100 ml) chicken or vegetable
  broth
¼ tsp salt
1 tsp sesame oil

PREPARATION

- Wash the pea shoots thoroughly. Bash the garlic with the flat side of a knife or cleaver and remove the skin. Mince the garlic and place in a small bowl or ramekin.

- Put the sauce ingredients in a bowl and mix well.

�֎ BUILD YOUR WOK CLOCK: place your chopped garlic at 12 o'clock, then arrange the pea shoots and sauce bowl clockwise around the plate.

COOKING

- Heat the vegetable oil in a wok over high heat until smoking-hot. Add the garlic, immediately followed by the pea shoots, and stir-fry for 30 seconds until the garlic is fragrant.

- Pour the sauce ingredients into the wok and bring to a vigorous boil. Cook for 1 minute until the pea shoots have wilted but are still vibrant in color. Serve immediately.

! TIP: If your sauce isn't thickening up properly, mix together 2 tsp of cornstarch with 2 Tbsp of cold water and stir it into your sauce before serving.

The Chinese do not like to overcook or overpower their greens as they really are the balancing act to what could otherwise be a very meat-filled, seafood-heavy meal. Simply blanch your greens (whichever you choose) and follow the timings below to provide the perfect counter to a proper Chinese meal.

GLAZED CHINESE GREENS WITH OYSTER SAUCE

SERVES: 2
PREPARATION TIME: 5 MINUTES
COOKING TIME: 5 MINUTES

10½ to 14 oz (300 to 400 g) Chinese greens (bok choy, choi sum, or Chinese broccoli)
½ Tbsp vegetable oil
1 Tbsp oyster sauce

PREPARATION
• Wash the vegetables thoroughly and leave whole.

COOKING
• Fill a large saucepan or wok with water and bring to a rapid boil.

• Add the vegetables to the pan and let boil for between 1 to 5 minutes until tender (see page 142 for specific vegetable cooking times). Drain and place on a large serving plate. Using a pair of sharp scissors, cut the vegetables into bite-size pieces (see Tip).

• Heat the vegetable oil in a small saucepan or wok until smoking-hot, then remove from the heat and pour over the top of the greens. Serve piping hot with the oyster sauce on the side.

! TIP: To add a bit of style to the presentation of this simple dish, I like to use a trick that is used in Chinese restaurants; line up your whole-cooked vegetables neatly on a plate, then run a pair of scissors through them and cut into bite-size chunks, trying to keep the vegetables aligned so that they still look whole. This makes the dish a bit more interesting visually as well as making it easier to eat.

SWAPSIES: Instead of using water, try boiling the vegetables in chicken or vegetable broth to add a little extra flavor.

No matter what type of pickle you're making, bear in mind that the idea is to have an intense hit of sour, sweet, and salty in every bite. The next tip is to use vegetables that have both a good bite and absorb flavor well—whether crunchy or fibrous. Here the carrot and daikon provide excellent texture as well as a great contrast in color, and are guaranteed to look appetizing on the side of any meal.

PICKLED CARROT AND DAIKON

SERVES: 4
PREPARATION TIME: 20 MINUTES
PICKLING TIME: MINIMUM 1 HOUR

½ daikon
1 carrot

The Pickling Liquid
Generous 1 cup (250 ml) warm water
3 Tbsp distilled vinegar
  or rice vinegar
3 Tbsp superfine sugar
2 Tbsp salt

- Peel the daikon and carrot and cut into matchsticks.

- Mix the pickle ingredients together in a large bowl until the sugar and salt have dissolved.

- Fill a clean, tight-lidded jar, bowl, or lidded container with the carrot and daikon matchsticks and pour over the pickling mixture until the veg are fully covered and the container is full. Pop on the lid and let pickle for a minimum of 1 hour for immediate use, or up to 3 days for maximum flavor.

SWAPSIES: If you can't find daikon, switch it for 10½ oz (300 g) of any type of available radish.

Lotus root is essentially a natural filter—its porous texture absorbs flavor and moisture, making it easy to pickle. The best thing about pickling lotus root is that it keeps its crunch and has an earthy taste, which holds and complements the flavor of the pickling liquid. Adding the spinach accentuates that earthiness, while its contrasting softness brings out the lotus root's great texture.

PICKLED LOTUS ROOT AND SPINACH

SERVES: 4
PREPARATION TIME: 20 MINUTES
PICKLING TIME: MINIMUM 45 MINUTES

1 x 3¼- to 4-in (8- to 10-cm) lotus
  root stick
3½ oz (100 g) Chinese spinach or baby
  spinach leaves

The Pickling Liquid
10 Tbsp Chinkiang black
  rice vinegar
8 Tbsp superfine sugar
2 Tbsp salt
7 Tbsp (100 ml) hot water
4 Tbsp sesame oil
3 star anise
20 Sichuan peppercorns,
  lightly crushed
4 garlic cloves, finely sliced

- Mix all the pickling liquid ingredients together in a bowl until the sugar is fully dissolved.

- Bring a saucepan filled with water to a boil. Peel and cut the lotus root into ¹⁄₁₆-in (2-mm) slices, then add to the pan and blanch for 3 minutes. Remove from the pan and cool under running cold water, then drain.

- Fill a clean, tight-lidded jar, bowl, or lidded container with the blanched lotus root and spinach leaves and pour over the pickling mixture until the veg are fully covered and the container is full. Pop on the lid and let pickle for a minimum of 45 minutes for immediate use, or up to 1 day for maximum flavor.

! **TIP:** Lotus root tends to come in vacuum packs containing 3 to 4 root segments, which would probably be too much for just one recipe. To stop any going to waste, try making this recipe alongside the Five-Spice Lotus Leaf Chicken with Chinese Sausage (see page 100).

As rice is a staple food, potatoes are rarely seen in Chinese cooking. Too many starches or carbohydrates added to the plate or the table and the balance of a meal is affected. This dish, however, is very light and is often found as a side in specialist dumpling restaurants in different parts of China and Hong Kong. The gentle pickling of the potato gives it a crunchy texture, which provides a lovely, light contrasting bite to a bowl of dumplings and soup.

PICKLED POTATO

SERVES: 4
PREPARATION TIME: 20 MINUTES
PICKLING TIME: MINIMUM 1 HOUR

1 scallion
4 dried red chiles
2 garlic cloves, minced
Sea salt
8¾ oz (250 g) waxy potato (baby potatoes work well)

The Pickling Mixture
2 Tbsp rice vinegar
1 Tbsp light soy sauce
1 tsp granulated sugar
½ tsp sesame oil

- Cut the scallion into fine matchsticks. Put the red chiles in a bowl, cover with hot water, and let soak for 15 minutes. Drain, then coarsely chop.

- Mince the garlic. Using a mortar and pestle (or alternatively, the flat side of a knife), grind it together with a pinch of sea salt into a paste.

- Bring a saucepan filled with water to a boil. Peel the potatoes and slice them into fine matchsticks, then add to the pan along with 1 tsp of salt and blanch for 1 minute. Remove from the pan and cool under running cold water, then drain.

- Mix all the pickling liquid ingredients together in a bowl until the sugar is fully dissolved.

- Fill a clean tight-lidded jar, bowl, or lidded container with the potato matchsticks, scallion, chiles, and garlic paste, then pour over the pickling mixture until the veg are fully covered and the container is full. Pop on the lid and let pickle for a minimum of 1 hour for immediate use, or up to 2 days for maximum flavor.

SERVING SUGGESTION: This fresh pickle is fantastic for adding a crunch to a bowl of blanched or steamed dumplings. If you fancy an alternative light lunch with bold chinese flavors, try this dish with a portion of the Steamed Wontons in Chili Broth (see page 84).

Although it is not necessarily typical to eat raw vegetables in most parts of China, some of our traditional greens hold a great deal of flavor and make great simple salads like this one. Kai choi and bok choy are both from the mustard family—when eaten raw they have a slightly peppery and distinct mustardy flavor which goes very well with the bittersweet tastes of the radish and daikon. Adding the pickled carrot and daikon to the salad gives the dish a nice extra variation of texture, though it is not essential if you're in a hurry.

MUSTARD GREEN AND BOK CHOY SALAD

SERVES: 2
PREPARATION TIME: 20 MINUTES

3½ oz (100 g) kai choi (Chinese
  mustard greens)
3½ oz (100 g) bok choy
3 dried wood ear mushroom florets,
  soaked and drained (see page 47)
A large handful of cilantro
3 to 4 radishes
3 Tbsp sesame seeds
½ daikon
1¾ oz (50 g) Pickled Carrot and Daikon
  (see page 148)

The Dressing
1 garlic clove
A small piece of ginger
1 Tbsp sesame paste
4 Tbsp fresh lime juice
1 Tbsp light soy sauce
1 Tbsp granulated sugar
2 tsp sesame oil
A pinch of salt

- Chop the garlic and ginger and place in a bowl. Add the rest of the dressing ingredients and mix together until smooth.

- Coarsely chop the kai choi, bok choy, wood ear mushroom, and cilantro. Finely slice the radishes.

- Toast the sesame seeds in a dry wok for 2 to 3 minutes until fragrant and golden brown, then set aside.

- Bring a saucepan filled with water to a boil. Peel the daikon and cut it into fine slices, then add to the pan and blanch for 1 minute. Remove from the pan and cool under running cold water, then drain.

- Combine all the salad ingredients except the sesame seeds, cover with the dressing, and toss until evenly coated. Sprinkle over the sesame seeds and serve.

↺ **SWAPSIES:** If you can't get your hands on sesame paste, replace it with the same quantity of tahini.

*Mung bean vermicelli are a type of glass noodle
and become almost transparent when cooked.
They provide a slightly "jellylike" bite to a dish and
a great texture for salads and soups. Light, fresh,
and healthy-tasting, this is one salad I could happily
eat for lunch every day, though it also works well
as a dinner party side or as an accompaniment to a
summer barbecue.*

GLASS NOODLE
CHICKEN SALAD

SERVES: 4
PREPARATION TIME: 30 MINUTES

3½ oz (100 g) mung bean vermicelli
3½ oz (100 g) chicken breast or thigh
½ carrot
½ cucumber
2 scallions
1 Tbsp sesame seeds

The Dressing
2 Tbsp light soy sauce
1½ tsp Chinkiang black rice vinegar
1½ tsp granulated sugar
1 Tbsp chicken broth
1 Tbsp sesame paste
2 Tbsp chili oil
½ tsp Sichuan peppercorns, crushed
1 tsp sesame oil

- Put the mung bean vermicelli in a bowl, cover with hot water, and let soak for 5 minutes until the noodles have softened but are still al dente. Remove from the water and let dry on a clean dish towel.

- Bring a saucepan filled with water to a boil, add the chicken, and poach for 7 to 10 minutes, or until cooked through. Remove from the pan, drain, and slice into thin shreds.

- Cut the carrot, cucumber, and scallions into fine matchsticks.

- Toast the sesame seeds in a dry wok until fragrant and golden brown (about 2 to 3 minutes), then set aside.

- Put all the dressing ingredients in a small bowl and mix together well.

- Place all the salad ingredients except the sesame seeds in a separate bowl, pour over the dressing, and mix together until everything is evenly coated. Transfer the dressed salad to a serving plate and sprinkle over the toasted sesame seeds to finish. Serve.

SWAPSIES: Try varying this dish by switching the noodles for sweet potato, spinach, or cassava noodles instead.

INDEX

First published in 2015 by Quadrille Publishing Limited

Text © Jeremy Pang 2015
Design and layout © Quadrille Publishing Ltd 2015
Photography © Martin Poole 2015
Illustration © Freya Jones 2015

Quadrille is an imprint of Hardie Grant
www.hardiegrant.com.au

Quadrille Publishing Limited
Pentagon House
52–54 Southwark Street
London SE1 1UN
www.quadrille.com

ISBN 978 184949 837 1

British Library Cataloguing-in-Publication Data. A catalogue
record for this book is available from the British Library.

Publishing Director: Jane O'Shea
Creative Director: Helen Lewis
Project Editor: Simon Davis
Designer: Nicola Ellis
Illustrator: Freya Jones
Photographer: Martin Poole
Food Stylists: Emily Jonzen, Camilla Baynham
Props Stylist: Iris Bromet
Production: Emily Noto and Vincent Smith

Printed and bound in China

ACKNOWLEDGEMENTS

First of all, I'd like to thank my wife Dee, for being my best friend and life partner and coming up with the School of Wok idea in the first place. Thanks for always humoring my crazy ideas, but mostly for sticking by me and helping me to nurture the best ones.

My dear Mum, our talents would never have developed without your relentless teaching, pushing, constant determination and endless love. And to your heavenly barbecue pork recipe, which now has the chance to sit on more coffee tables than you could ever imagine.

To my dad, for inspiring me to cook and teaching me that there is more to breakfast, lunch and dinner than just eating and that the snacks in between those meals are just as important, if not a million times more fun. And to my sisters Wendy and Jennifer, for sharing every morsel of those snacks with me since we were kids.

Nev Leaning, my business partner, for believing in me from the start, opposing me when I need to hear it, making massive decisions in business together and generally being my honorary Chinese chuckle brother.

Team School of Wok (Stefan Lind, Melissa Wong, Hannah Dryden-Jones, Ali Price,

Yolanda Irais Ocon and Johnathon Campbell) for their consistent passion not just for food but also for our ever-growing success at School of Wok. You guys wok my world!

A huge thanks to Adrienne Katz Kennedy for also being a crucial member of our team, but more importantly for playing a massive part in editing all my wok waffle before the book even reached the publisher. Thanks to her persistence, beady-eyed work on the manuscript and her ability to both encourage and criticise simultaneously – a unique skill to have.

To Freya Jones from The Brand New Studio for working so closely with School of Wok and I from the start and for creating such wonderful illustrations for the book.

To Borra Garson and Jan Croxon for introducing me to Quadrille and to Luisa Welch for helping to push me forward. And to everyone at Quadrille who has made this journey so enjoyable: Jane O'Shea, Simon Davis, Nikki Ellis, Ed Griffiths, Helen Lewis, Martin Poole, Faith Mason, Iris Bromet, Camilla Baynham, Emily Jonzen and Wilson Chung. Wow! What a team. Let's hope for more to come!